T0248302

TECHNIQUES AND TIPS FOR
COVERING CAKES

Claire Fitzsimons

TECHNIQUES AND TIPS FOR
COVERING CAKES

THE CROWOOD PRESS

CONTENTS

• • • • • • • •

PREFACE

. . . . . .

I have been teaching, in some form or another, for nearly forty years. I began my teaching career in London as a primary school teacher, and taught for nearly twenty-five years before embarking on a change of direction.

Cooking and baking have always been centre stage in my life. My parents and grandparents were all good cooks, and I was always keen to be in the kitchen, amongst all the action! My Nana, who lived with us, started collecting a monthly magazine called the *Cordon Bleu Cookery Course*. When the magazines were reprinted into a collection of twelve books, she bought me the set for my sixteenth birthday. My love for cooking and baking was then firmly established. When I left home to go to college, my books came with me. Whilst I was teaching cooking, baking and sugarcraft became my hobby and creative outlet, and I attended a variety of weekend courses, mostly sugarcraft and cake decorating.

When my husband and I decided to move away from London, I knew I would need to occupy myself with something if I was not going to be in the classroom every day. Sitting at the kitchen table one night, my husband looked up at my cookery books and pointed to my Cordon Bleu books. 'How about going on a course there?' Before I had an opportunity to change my mind, I had enrolled on a three-month course! The three months became nine months and I qualified as a Chef de Cuisine in the summer of 2007. I then completed a part-time Sugarcraft course at Brooklands College in Weybridge.

After working as a private chef and wedding-cake maker for a while, I began to miss teaching. I applied to work as a sugarcraft tutor in a renowned cookery school in Farnham, Surrey. I taught general sugarcraft skills, making wired sugar flowers and baking. I also became a cookery tutor for Surrey adult learning, teaching French cuisine. When the Covid pandemic struck, both schools were forced to close. As life started to slowly return to normal, I made the decision to continue to teach, but only at home. I now run small sugarcraft workshops from my home in Surrey.

There has been a resurgence of interest in cake making and decorating in recent years, mainly due to popular television programmes such as *The Great British Bake Off*. The internet and a variety of publications all provide recipes, along with a photograph of the finished cake. In this book I provide practical step-by-step guidance, using simple instructions and photographs that describe how to cover a variety of cakes using six different types of cake covering, as well as a photograph of the finished cake.

Chapters 3 to 6 each include three projects of differing complexity. I have included some simple recipes for the cakes, but as the focus of this book is on how to cover the cakes, most of the detailed instructions are about the covering. Popular cake coverings such as buttercream and chocolate are included, as well as sugarpaste and royal icing. Some of the cake coverings are quick to do, but I have also included projects that require some time and preparation.

My final chapter gives an assortment of ideas for final decorations. I have called it 'Finishing Touches'. Many of these decorations can be bought ready-made, and when time is an issue this may be your preference. However, most of the decorations can be made well in advance and stored until needed. They could be 'mini projects' when time allows.

When the pandemic struck, I contemplated teaching online classes but decided it was not for me. About ten years ago one of my students, Kate, commented 'you have so many handy hints and tips – you should write a book!' So when I was approached by The Crowood Press, and remembering Kate's comment, I thought – why not? This would be a wonderful opportunity to teach and share my ideas in a different format.

Nothing has given me greater pleasure than teaching learners of all ages, sharing with them the skills needed and giving them the confidence to succeed.

I hope this book will give you all the guidance required to produce a beautifully covered cake!

CHAPTER 1

BASIC CAKE-DECORATING MATERIALS AND TOOLS

· ·

Before embarking on any kind of cake decorating, it is important to ensure you have the correct tools to hand. There are some essential pieces of equipment that all cake decorators will need, as well as specialised tools that are specific to the type of cake covering.

There is a dizzying array of equipment to buy on the market now, some of which are very useful, but many of which are not! Buying good, well-made materials and tools from reputable companies will be more cost effective in the long run as they will last for years. Tools that are cheap to buy and promise a 'quick fix' decoration rarely deliver.

This chapter will act as a guide through some of the items used for cake covering, beginning with the essential pieces of equipment. The chapter later looks at some items that may be useful to have, but are not necessarily vital!

ESSENTIAL EQUIPMENT

Cake Tins

Cake tins come in all shapes and sizes, from round, square and rectangular, to loaf and hemisphere. Unless the plan is to have a career in cake making, consider the practicalities

Some essential tools for cake decorating.

Cake tins come in all shapes and sizes.

of storing a huge collection, as well as the issue of the cost. Rather than purchasing an array of tins, buy just one or two good quality tins of a standard size instead.

Most family cake recipes call for a 20cm (8in) round deep tin. This size will give approximately fourteen cake servings. This is useful if you are considering baking a tall sponge cake with several layers of buttercream or ganache.

A smaller, 15cm (6in) tin will be large enough for a sponge celebration cake serving six to eight people.

Popular tins include:

- **Shallow sandwich tins**: These are useful for making a layered cake. The advantage here is that cakes are quicker to bake, the disadvantage being that more than one tin will be needed. Tins that have a removable bottom are useful as cakes are easier to remove from the tin.
- **Spring-form tins:** These have a spring-loaded clip at the side of the tin. This makes the removal of delicate cream sponges or cheesecakes much easier.
- **Loaf tins:** These tins usually come in two sizes, 450g (1lb) and 900g (2lb), although the shapes of the tins can vary from quite narrow with sharp corners to square with rounded corners. These are used for loaves, sweet and savoury.
- **Square and rectangular tins:** These tins are popular for celebration cakes. They have the advantage of making a cake that is much easier to portion up. This might be a consideration if tasked with cutting up a large cake at a party.

  Another cake for large events and parties is the popular traybake. There are traybake tins available to buy, but a sharp-cornered roasting tin could be used instead.
- **Bundt tins:** These tins have become increasingly popular. They produce very ornate, patterned cakes that require minimal or even no cake covering. This can be a huge advantage if time is short. They are available to buy in both metal and flexible silicone, and come in a variety of shapes and sizes. The most expensive to buy are made from cast aluminium. They are quite heavy, but have

the advantages of producing a cake with well-defined patterns, and being able to withstand many years of use. The advantage of silicone moulds is that they are much cheaper to buy, however, the detail on the finished bake often lacks definition.

- **Novelty cake tins:** These tins have become increasingly popular, particularly for children's cakes. The results can sometimes be disappointing as the impressed pattern on the inside of the tin is rarely defined and is often lost on the baked cake. Consider buying a shaped tin instead. A dome or hemisphere tin, for example, would give far more decorating opportunities, from making a ladybird cake or 'the skirt' on a doll cake, to a spaceman's helmet or even a football!

Whichever cake tin is used, always remember to prepare the tin correctly, either by greasing and/or lining it with good quality baking paper. This will not only help to release the cake, but it will also extend the life of the tin.

Stand Mixer

A stand mixer should not be considered an essential piece of equipment. Most good stand mixers are extremely expensive, and it is perfectly possible to make all the coverings in this book without using one. But if you enjoy baking it is a worthwhile investment. A good quality machine can last many years. Most brands come with useful attachments, including a paddle for mixing batters as well as a whisk for whipping cream and egg-based toppings. Kenwood and KitchenAid are two of the most popular brands. Both have different sized models with differing capacities, and both have various add-on attachments available. These machines are often available to buy second hand or as 'reconditioned'.

A stand mixer and hand whisk are both useful for a keen cake maker.

Hiring Tins

If a very large tin or a novelty shaped pan is needed for a one-off event, consider hiring one from a local cake-decorating shop. Second-hand tins are also available to buy in charity shops and from online sites such as eBay.

Hand Mixer

A hand mixer is another kitchen appliance to consider. As it is more compact and affordable than a stand mixer, it is a very useful alternative. Many cake makers believe a lighter sponge can be achieved by using a hand mixer rather than the more powerful stand machine, which may overbeat more delicate cake mixtures. Most have a set of attachments, including a whisk. These vary enormously in price, and it is worth doing a little research to find one that best suits your needs as well as your budget. Some hand mixers are available with a stand. Also new to the market are cordless machines, which would be very useful when whisking in a confined space or when needing to whisk a mixture over a bain marie or near to the cooker.

Weighing Scales

Weighing ingredients accurately is essential when following a recipe, so a reliable set of scales is a worthwhile investment. Digital scales tend to be the most accurate, and most allow measurements to be changed between imperial and metric. Salter are a trusted brand, but there are many on the market to suit every budget.

Cake Turntable

A revolving turntable is an essential piece of decorating equipment. It will allow the cake to be turned round with one hand whilst applying the covering of buttercream, ganache or whatever with the other. It will raise the cake to a workable height, which will help to avoid neck and back strain. It will also make it easier to check that the cake is level.

Avoid using a static cake stand with a lipped edge for decorating. These are for displaying and presenting a finished cake. A decorating turntable has a flat edge, making it easier to slide the cake off the surface. Some have a non-slip surface and have a 'tilt' facility. This is very useful when piping small and delicate details round the sides of a cake.

Serrated Knife or Cake-Cutting Wire

A long serrated knife, such as a bread or ham knife, is useful to cut cakes across for even layers. A serrated knife will cut through a sponge without tearing it. Another option is to use a cake-cutting wire. These are easy to use and inexpensive. The next chapter will explain how to use both a serrated knife and a cutting wire to level a cake, as well as slice it into even layers for filling.

Non-Stick Rolling Pin

When covering a cake with marzipan or sugarpaste, a rolling pin will be needed. For cake decorating, these are usually made from silicone or plastic rather than wood, as they need to be non-stick. They come in a variety of sizes. Choose one that is an appropriate length for the width of the cake.

Non-Stick Board or Rolling Mat

A non-stick board or silicone rolling mat will make the task of rolling out marzipan or sugarpaste so much easier. It will reduce the amount of icing sugar or cornflour used when trying to prevent the paste from sticking to the work surface. If space is an issue, consider having a silicone roll-up

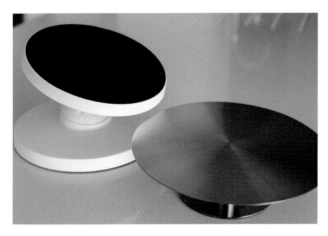

Examples of static and tilting turntables.

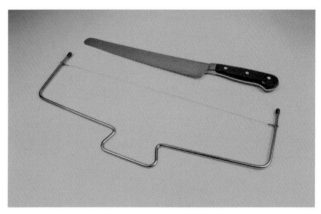

A long serrated knife or cake wire cutter is useful for cutting cakes into even layers.

mat. They are non-slip and come in a variety of sizes. Buy a large one that will give a spacious working area. Some have measurements and size guides printed on them, which will help when rolling out the paste.

Cake Boards and Cake Drums

Cake boards are available in a variety of shapes and sizes and are inexpensive to buy. They are needed not only to display decorated cakes, but also to give a support under each cake when making a tiered or stacked cake. Cake drums are non-compressed cake boards. They usually have a depth of approximately 1cm (0.4in). When covering a drum with sugarpaste, the combined depth of the paste and the drum equals 15mm (0.6in), so the edge of the board can be covered with 15mm-width ribbon.

Large disposable food-safe boards are useful when decorating. They make the task of moving a fragile cake from work surface to turntable or display board so much easier. If a cake board is not used underneath the cake when moving it, there is a high chance that it will crack when being lifted into position.

Baking or Parchment Paper

Baking paper has several uses for cake decorating as well as the more obvious use as a wrapping. Once baked cakes have cooled, they need to be covered. A good quality baking paper or non-stick parchment paper will prevent the cakes from drying out. It is available to buy on a roll, as sheets, or as ready-cut circles. The ready-cut circles are particularly useful when needing to line several tins for baking. Baking

parchment can be used for making piping bags for royal icing. Small squares of baking paper or waxed paper are required when using a flower nail for piping flowers with buttercream, royal icing or ganache. Simple stencils for decorating the sides and top of a frosted cake can also be made with baking paper.

Aluminium Foil

Foil is another essential item and one that most people have in their kitchen cupboard. Foil has several uses. As well as being used in baking, it is perfect for wrapping cakes such as fruit cakes for long-term storage. It can also be scrunched up or moulded into cups to use as a mould for drying sugar and chocolate decorations.

Acetate Sheets and Rolls

Food-safe acetate sheets are readily available to buy online or in specialist cake and sugarcraft stores. They are invaluable for piping small decorations with royal icing and chocolate. Acetate is also available to buy on a roll in various widths. Narrow-width rolls are often referred to as cake collars. Here the acetate can be used either to line a cake tin to give extra height, or to support creamy fillings before setting when making a cold dessert or a cake such as a Frasier.

When working with melted chocolate, a strip of acetate can also be used to apply a side design to a cake. Once set, the acetate can be peeled away easily without having to touch the surface decoration. The chocolate will have a smooth sheen devoid of finger marks!

Spatulas

A set of rubber or silicone spatulas are handy to have for mixing small quantities of icing, buttercream or jam. Silicone ones can withstand high temperatures. They are easy to clean, which is a huge advantage when mixing syrups and sticky glazes.

Palette Knives

A large, long palette knife is very useful for applying various coatings to the top and sides of cakes with a large surface. A small-angled palette knife allows coating or icing to be applied to hard-to-reach areas whilst keeping hands and fingers away from the icing.

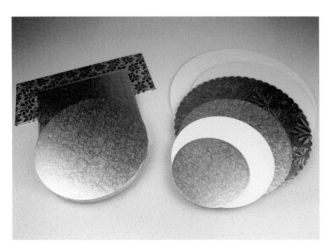

Cake boards and cake drums are available in a variety of shapes and sizes.

Palette knives – long, short and angled.

Tape Measure or Ruler

Measuring the depth and diameter of the cake is necessary before rolling out marzipan or sugarpaste. Guesswork is not an option here, and having something to measure with will save time and avoid a potentially costly mistake!

Rolling-Pin Guide Rings and Spacers

A quick and easy way to achieve an even thickness when rolling out marzipan and sugarpaste is to use either rolling-pin guide rings or spacers. The silicone guide rings have two rings in each set and are used by attaching one ring to each end of the rolling pin and then rolling out the paste until the guide rings touch the work surface. The advantage of the set of ring guides is that they come in different thicknesses so can be used for pastry as well as marzipan and sugarpaste.

The set of two spacers is used by placing one on each side of your paste and rolling out until the rolling pin no longer spreads the paste and the correct depth of paste is achieved.

Cake Smoothers

If covering a cake with marzipan or sugarpaste, a cake smoother is an essential tool – and ideally use two, one for each hand. Choose smoothers that have at least one straight edge with sharp corners. They are used to smooth the paste on the top and sides of the cake. They can also give a polished finish to sugarpaste. Flexible smoothers are used when decorating cakes with sharp edges. They are made of silicone and come in various shapes and sizes.

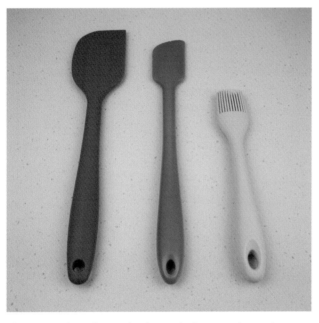

Silicone spatulas and pastry brushes are both easy to clean and can withstand high heat.

Silicone Pastry Brush

Traditional pastry brushes are made with natural bristles and usually a wooden handle. They are used for applying glazes or an egg wash. They are difficult to clean thoroughly as they require handwashing only. In time they will also begin to shed their bristles. Silicone pastry brushes on the other hand are heatproof, dishwasher safe and do not shed their bristles. They are more hygienic as they can be cleaned at a higher temperature, avoiding a build-up of old food particles.

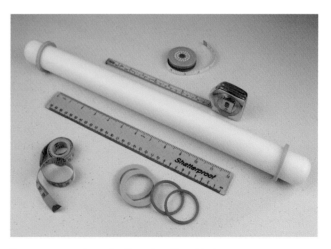

Tape measure, ruler and rolling-pin with guide rings.

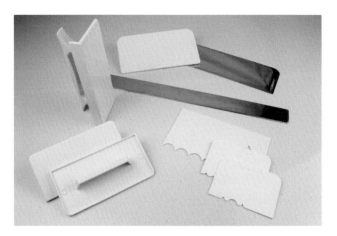
Cake smoothers, side scrapers and contour combs.

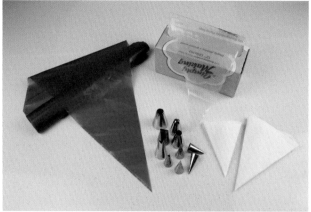
Different sized piping bags and a variety of piping nozzles.

Side Scrapers and Contour Combs

These tools are used to scrape away excess buttercream, royal icing, chocolate or ganache, as well as giving a final smooth coating to a cake. They are available in plastic and metal, and both work equally well. However, metal scrapers can be used warm, which can sometimes be helpful when wanting to achieve a smooth buttercream, ganache or chocolate coating.

Side scrapers come in different sizes, so think about the height of the finished cake. Tall side scrapers are available to buy for modern, multiple-layered cakes. Double-edged scrapers, also known as contour combs, have either one straight side and one patterned side, or two patterned sides. These can be used with buttercream, chocolate ganache or royal icing to create contours and patterns on the sides of cakes.

Piping Bags

For piping buttercream and ganache, some large piping bags will be needed. This size of piping bag is available either as a reusable bag that is usually made of nylon or silicone, or as a disposable bag, made of plastic. These are usually sold on a roll and are less cost effective but are sometimes preferred as they are more convenient. Good quality plastic bags are easier to grip when piping, they can be washed thoroughly, and reused several times before disposal. Biodegradable plastic bags are also now readily available.

Buttercream- and ganache-filled bags can also be stored in the fridge or freezer.

Paper piping bags are used for piping small quantities of royal icing or chocolate. These can be bought ready-made in various sizes, as well as in sheets, ready cut to assemble into bags. The most cost-effective option is to make a piping bag, using good quality baking parchment. Easy step-by-step instructions on how to make one can be found on p.102.

Piping Nozzles

Choosing the correct piping nozzle is dependent on the type of decoration required. Larger nozzles are made of either metal or plastic and are generally used for piping buttercream and other thick frostings. Small metal piping nozzles are used for royal icing or melted chocolate. Most nozzles are identified by a number or letter, although some brands prefer to use their own numbering system, which can be rather confusing! There are some specific nozzles required in the projects for buttercream and royal icing, and examples of piping effects given in Chapter 9.

USEFUL EQUIPMENT

Pizza Wheel

A pizza wheel is not an essential cake-decorating piece of equipment, but a kitchen tool that many households may already own. It is very useful for easily trimming away marzipan and sugarpaste around the base of the cake once it is covered.

Small Spirit Level

Although not an essential piece of equipment, a small spirit level can be extremely useful. A level cake will be much easier to cover, and is vital when stacking cakes one on top of another. Keep a small spirit level just for cake decorating.

Cake Cooling Rack

As well as using a cooling rack for cooling down baked cakes, a rack will be needed when applying drips and liquid glazes to a cake. Choose a cooling rack that has a non-stick coating. It will be easier to remove the cake from the rack as well as being easier to clean.

Kitchen Thermometer

An easy-to-read digital hand-held thermometer with a long probe will take the guesswork out of checking the temperature of cooked frostings, such as ganache, Swiss meringue buttercream and mirror glazes. They are easily obtainable from most good cook shops.

Tweezers

This is another non-essential item, but one that can be extremely useful when applying tiny embellishments, such as tiny sugar pearls, on to a finished cake. Cake-decorating tweezers are usually curved to help place small decorations accurately anywhere on the cake without damaging the cake surface.

Fine Skewer, Scribing Tool and Acupuncture Needles

All these tools can be used for similar tasks when using sugarpaste as a cake covering.

Sometimes air bubbles form in the paste when rolling it out, and these can be easily removed using one of these tools. They are useful for accurately marking a guide line when piping on the side of a cake. They are also useful for marking on the top of the cake as a guide for inserting dowels when making a stacked cake.

A very fine skewer is easily available in most good cook-shops. A scribing tool is a cake-decorating tool that has a handle with a fine, needle-like tip. These are available from most good cake-decorating shops. Individually wrapped acupuncture needles are also a good choice as they are sterile and therefore more hygienic to use. They are easily available to buy online.

Shaped Cutters and Plunger Cutters

These cutters are certainly not essential, but when time is short and a quick decoration is needed on top of a cake, a little set of cutters is useful to have at hand. Plunger cutters such as these can provide an almost instant sugarpaste decoration with minimal effort. An example of their use can be found in Project 16 in Chapter 8.

Silicone Moulds

Small silicone moulds such as these can also give an instant impact to a finished cake. They are more expensive to buy than cutters, but sugarpaste, chocolate and marzipan can all be used in a silicone mould. Examples of their use can be found in Chapter 9, 'Finishing Touches'.

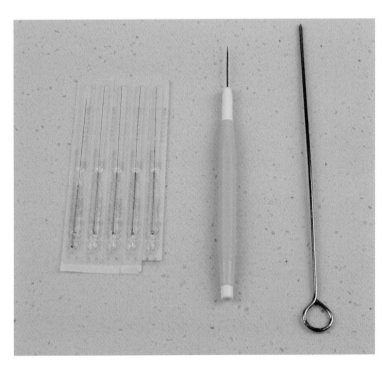

Acupuncture needles, scribing tool and a fine skewer.

A selection of shaped cutters and plunger cutters.

A variety of silicone moulds.

CHAPTER 2

CAKES – ALL SHAPES AND SIZES!

• •

There is a style and type of cake to suit every occasion! So, think about the event and how many servings will be needed. Also consider whether there might be any dietary requirements to take into account. Most recipes can now be easily adapted to make a gluten-free or vegan cake, thanks to readily available ingredients in the supermarket. If making a cake for a family celebration, consider the dietary restrictions for children, pregnant or nursing mums and elderly relatives. Using cake toppings that contain raw egg white or alcohol may not be appropriate.

As this book is about providing the tips and techniques needed for covering cakes, some cake recipes are not given, although the recipes for fillings and toppings have all been provided in the projects throughout the book. Here are some suggestions for popular cakes to suit a variety of occasions, as well as step-by-step instructions on how to

Consider Where the Event Will Take Place

If the party is outside and the cake is going to be sitting in the sunshine for longer than fifteen minutes, then a fresh cream filling or a cream cheese topping may not be a suitable choice!

A variety of cakes, all shapes and sizes.

prepare two types of sponge cake for filling and covering. One is a round sponge, baked in two separate sandwich tins, and the other is a rolled fatless sponge.

VICTORIA SANDWICH

A Victoria sandwich is a perennial favourite when filled with jam and/or buttercream or freshly whipped cream. A simple finish can be made by dusting with either icing sugar or caster sugar. To make a very simple decorative topping use either a stencil or paper doily. Place this on the top of the cake before dusting over lightly with icing or caster sugar as shown in the step-by-step guide below.

A basic recipe for a Victoria sandwich, sometimes known as a Victoria sponge, can also be adapted to make other flavoured cakes, using any of the citrus fruits. Fresh lemon, lime, orange and grapefruit all work well by adding the zest of the fruits into the cake mixture and the juice to a buttercream filling. Avoid adding juice to fresh cream fillings as they will curdle. Both chocolate and coffee cakes can also be made using a Victoria sandwich recipe. For a chocolate cake, substitute some of the flour in the cake recipe with cocoa powder, or make a paste by mixing cocoa powder with water or milk and add melted chocolate to the buttercream filling. Coffee essence or reconstituted coffee granules can be added to both the cake batter as well as the buttercream filling. Adding walnuts to coffee cakes is also a popular choice, but best avoided if young children will be eating the cake.

When making a selection of cakes for large gatherings, it is also a good idea to label specific cakes if they contain ingredients known to cause allergic reactions, such as nuts and sesame seeds. As well as baking larger cakes, consider making individual cakes using cupcake paper cases or individual card cases, either round or loaf shaped.

MADEIRA CAKE

Madeira cake has a denser, closer texture than a Victoria sandwich or Swiss roll. It is a popular recipe for wedding cakes that require more intricate and time-consuming decorations as it will keep for a much longer period of time, without the need for freezing. Madeira cakes can be filled and covered with either buttercream or ganache, and then iced with sugarpaste. As the sponge is quite dense and firm, it is popular when cakes need to be stacked one on top of another to create a tiered cake. How to prepare and stack a three-tiered cake is demonstrated in Project 18 in Chapter 8.

FATLESS SPONGE

This recipe is used for making light sponge layers for fresh cream gâteaux and Swiss rolls, as well as sponge bases for fruit flans and Frasier sponges. They are best baked, filled and served on the same day, but they do freeze well. These sponges are sometimes referred to as Genoese, but some

A Victoria sandwich cake.

A Swiss roll made with a fatless sponge.

Genoese recipes contain melted butter. Fatless sponge bases are easily available to buy ready-made, but due to the recent baking revival, and an increased awareness of the provenance of ingredients, many bakers prefer to make their own.

A flan tin will be needed. This looks similar to a tart tin but has a raised middle so that when the sponge is turned out from the tin it has a deep rim surrounding the base to encase the filling and topping. It can then be filled with either fresh or patisserie cream, and topped with fresh fruits or berries. A simple glaze brushed on to the fruit will give an attractive finish and will also enhance and preserve the colour of the fruits. Step-by-step instructions for filling and topping a Swiss roll are given later in this chapter.

GENOESE SPONGE

A Genoese sponge is a very light but firm sponge. It is made by whisking eggs and sugar together to create a mousse-like mixture, before carefully folding in flour followed by melted butter. It is a classic teatime favourite and is best served filled with fresh summer fruits and whipped cream. This type of cake could also be decorated with a dusting of icing sugar.

CARROT CAKE

Carrot cake has become a very popular cake with all ages, and is often requested for wedding cakes. It has a moist, open texture and keeps well as the fat used in the recipe is usually oil rather than butter. The classic topping is a cream-cheese buttercream, which does reduce the keeping time of the cake if not kept refrigerated. White chocolate buttercream or ganache with the addition of some fresh orange zest would be a delicious alternative filling and topping for a carrot cake that requires a longer shelf life.

How to Prepare a Sponge Cake for Filling and Decorating

Any type of sponge cake recipe can be used for this quick, easy method of filling and topping. If the cake has been baked in one deep tin, then it will need to be cut across into two halves. This is a Victoria sandwich, baked in two separate sandwich tins and filled with raspberry jam and Chantilly cream.

Level the cake that will be used as the bottom layer, if it has a domed top. Cut with either a long bread knife with a serrated edge, or a cake leveller.

Carefully lift the bottom cake and place it on a cake board or a serving plate. Spread some jam on the top of the bottom cake.

3

Fill a large piping bag with Chantilly cream fitted with a piping nozzle. Wilton 6B has been used here, but any large piping nozzle can be used for this.

4

Pipe small rosettes round the edge of the bottom layer. Gently squeeze the piping bag from the top of the bag to form the rosette, then stop squeezing and immediately lift it up before moving on to the next rosette. Try and pipe the rosettes so they are roughly the same size.

5

Now swirl the remainder of the cream into the middle of the cake. Carefully place the second cake on the top. Refrigerate until ready to decorate.

6

Place the stencil or doily on the cake. Use either pearl-headed dressmaker pins or cocktail sticks to secure it on the cake if necessary.

7

Use either a sugar duster or sieve to apply a light coating of icing sugar to the surface. Do not be tempted to over dust as the pattern will smudge when the stencil or doily is lifted away from the cake.

8

Serve the cake as soon as possible after dusting, as storing in the fridge will cause the icing sugar to dissolve and the pattern will disappear. This 'Forever Frost' icing will not dissolve as quickly on the cake surface.

LOAF CAKES

A loaf cake is a popular teatime treat. It is less fragile than a sponge, making it a good choice when the cake needs to be transported. It can be baked in a greaseproof liner so it is easy to remove from the tin, and the liner also provides a wrapping so there is no need for a box. It is an easy cake to cut into slices, which is convenient for a bake sale. Tea breads, such as bara brith, Yorkshire tea loaf and malt loaf, all contain dried fruits. They keep well and can be stored for up to a week without refrigeration, wrapped in foil. They can also be frozen.

Other popular loaf cakes such as lemon drizzle, cherry and almond do not keep for longer than a few days, but they freeze well for up to three months. These types of cake do not require a filling, but can be decorated with piped swirls of flavoured buttercream, or topped with a sugary crusty glaze before adding finishing touches such as glacé cherries, nuts, chocolate curls or sugar sprinkles.

Loaf cakes and tea bread.

TRAYBAKES

Traybakes are a popular choice for feeding a crowd. They can be baked and decorated all in one tin, and do not require a special tin. A roasting tin measuring approximately 30 × 25cm (12 × 10in) can be used, if it is lined with baking paper. They do not require a filling; however, if a very large cake is required, then two layers can be baked and sandwiched together with a filling. Any flavoured buttercream can be used to pipe a decorative topping.

INDIVIDUAL CAKES

Individual or mini cakes are a popular choice for buffet parties as well as wedding favours. They are more elegant than cupcakes, and can be decorated to compliment a larger cake by using the same filling, topping and decoration. A specialist tin that has individual recesses each with a loose bottom is required so that the cakes bake evenly and can be easily removed from the tin without damaging the sides. They can then be halved and filled in the same way as a larger cake.

Traybakes.

Individual cakes.

CUPCAKES

Cupcakes are easy to prepare, as they are usually baked in paper cases or baking cups, so greasing and lining cake tins is not required. Due to their size, they are also quick to bake. They can be filled with buttercream and topped with either more buttercream, icing, frosting, ganache or chocolate. Choose from a wide variety of decorations such as sugarpaste or chocolate shapes, glacé fruits, sugar sprinkles or edible flowers to give a final embellishment.

Cupcake wrappers or collars come in a range of designs and can be used for either a finishing touch for themed children's parties, or to serve cupcakes when used as favours for a wedding or an anniversary celebration. Baking cups have the advantage of being used as both a baking case as well as providing a decorative finish. They are also sturdier when having to transport them to a venue, or when placed in the freezer for long-term storage.

Cupcakes.

> **Baking Tip!**
>
> When baking individual cupcakes, place a few grains of rice into the tin under the cases, before filling with the cake mixture. The rice will absorb any grease, leaving the cases unmarked.
>
> Remember to remove the cases from the tin as soon as they come out of the oven: this will prevent the cases from peeling away from the cakes.

BUNDT AND SAVARIN RING CAKES

Bundt tins have become almost collectable items in recent times, due to the intricate patterns and details that can be created on the cake. Minimal decoration is required other than a drizzle of icing or chocolate. A savarin is a ring-shaped tin, available in various sizes. They create an elegant cake, which is easy to cut into neat portions. Most popular cake recipes, such as for vanilla, chocolate or cherry cake, can be baked in either of these tins.

Bundt decorated with a drizzle of icing and sugar flowers.

SWISS ROLL OR ROULADE

A Swiss roll or roulade is a quick and easy cake to make, and can be simply decorated with a few swirls of buttercream or a drizzle of melted chocolate. It is made with a fatless sponge, so has a very light texture. It is best eaten on the day as it does not keep well. However, it can be filled and frozen and will keep in the freezer for up to three months. 'Roulade' simply means 'rolled' and is used to describe both savoury and sweet bakes using either pastry or sponge. When used to describe a cake, it is usually referring to a richer dessert recipe, often using fresh cream and flavoured with a liqueur. The method for rolling and filling a chocolate roulade to make a Yule log is given in Project 7 in Chapter 5.

FRUIT CAKES

There are many types of fruit cake, ranging from light tea loaves to spiced cakes with added dried fruits, such as a simnel or Dundee cake through to the dark, heavily fruited cakes laced with alcohol. A rich fruit cake is still a popular choice of cake for weddings, anniversaries, birthdays and other family celebrations, as well as annual festivities such as Christmas. It is usually regarded as the ultimate traditional celebration cake.

A fruit cake containing plenty of dried fruit and steeped with brandy, rum or another spirit, can be baked and stored away for months. It is usually covered with marzipan and icing, making it a perfect base for more intricate decorations such as piped royal icing and sugar flowers. However, in some regions of the country, particularly in Yorkshire, a rich fruit Christmas cake is traditionally served plain and undecorated, accompanied by some Wensleydale cheese.

Baking Tip!

If a rich fruit cake is required without alcohol, a mix of fresh lemon and orange juice can be used in place of the alcohol. It does not have the longer keeping qualities of an alcohol-infused cake, but it can still be made a few weeks in advance and stored until required. It must not be 'fed' with fruit juices as this will cause the cake to go mouldy.

How to Store and 'Feed' a Christmas Cake

The cake must be well wrapped, first in baking paper, then by a generous sheet of aluminium foil. Store in a cool, dry place. The cake will keep well for at least six months, but regularly 'feeding' the cake with additional alcohol will improve both the flavour and texture of the cake.

The popular method for adding extra alcohol is to finely skewer all over the surface of the cake before sparingly spooning over the alcohol. Alternatively, put the alcohol into a refillable spray bottle and 'mist' it over the surface of the cake without skewering it. This method is more hygienic and less likely to cause contamination to the cake. The alcohol can be stored in the bottle ready to use for the cake's weekly or fortnightly 'feed'.

Fruit cakes.

CHAPTER 3

BUTTERCREAM

• • • • • • • • • • • • •

uttercream is a popular choice for cake fillings and coverings. Most home bakers will have made the traditional American buttercream recipe, which consists of just butter and icing sugar as its main ingredients, but there are other less known recipes. Whilst most contain the same or similar ingredients of eggs, sugar and butter, they are each prepared differently and have different textures, flavours, consistencies and keeping qualities.

In this chapter there are three projects, each using one of the three most popular buttercreams: American, Swiss and Italian. However, any of the buttercreams described

Popular varieties of buttercream: from the left, American, Swiss and Italian.

in this chapter can be used for the projects. Each project includes a recipe for the buttercream as well as step-by-step instructions for making and using it. Although most of the recipes are quite straightforward, needing minimal ingredients, some do require more effort and time as well as specialist equipment, such as a stand mixer and sugar thermometer. Other less well-known buttercreams are also described in this chapter, as well as suggestions as to how they might be used for a particular cake.

When making any type of buttercream, buy the best ingredients available. A good quality unsalted butter bought in a block, with a high fat content of at least 82g (3oz) per 100g (3½oz), will produce the best consistency and flavour for buttercream. The advantage of using unsalted butter rather than salted is being able to control the amount of salt added to the buttercream. However, many prefer to use salted butter as it is believed to neutralise some of the sweetness. It is also sometimes cheaper than unsalted, and more likely to be used daily in most homes.

There are two types of icing sugar on the market. One is made from sugar beet and the other from sugar cane. Sugar beet is grown in the UK and therefore cheaper. It produces a slightly grainier buttercream. Icing sugar from sugar cane is more refined, giving a smoother buttercream. Both contain an anti-caking agent of either maize starch, potato starch or tricalcium phosphate. For American buttercream, the differences in the two sugars are not very discernible, but when making meringue-based buttercreams, cane sugar will produce a better, smoother result.

ADDING FLAVOURINGS TO BUTTERCREAM

All the different buttercream recipes can have additional flavours added to them. Citrus flavours such as lemon, orange and lime can be added to buttercream using either the zest or juice. Chocolate can be added to buttercream either by melting and cooling chocolate, or by adding cocoa powder. Coffee flavours can be added either by making a paste using freeze-dried coffee granules, using espresso powder, or by using a liquid coffee extract. Other flavours, such as vanilla and almond, are usually added by using an extract. Although there are many flavourings available in the supermarket, they are often described as an 'essence'. These are synthetic, chemically made flavourings and are usually much cheaper than natural extracts. Most larger supermarkets and cake-ingredient suppliers stock flavouring extracts, and it is worth paying a little more for this superior product as the flavour will be natural and more intense.

ADDING COLOUR TO BUTTERCREAM

As with flavourings, there are many different brands of food colouring on the market. Liquid colourings are readily available in the home baking section of most supermarkets. These are fine to use if only pastel or light colours are required. They are usually chemically produced and are often quite watery and weak, which entails having to use large quantities to produce a rich colour. Paste colours, which are very concentrated, are available from shops selling cake-making equipment, some craft stores, or online

Flavourings for buttercream.

This is a new product that has been developed to whiten buttercream.

ingredient and baking suppliers. These pastes are usually added to buttercream using the tip of a cocktail stick as they are so intense.

Liquid and paste colours are water or alcohol based and can be used to colour all buttercreams, icings and marzipan but must never be used for colouring chocolate, which requires an oil-based colourant.

Colourings for buttercream.

The easiest way to make white buttercream is to use a good quality unsalted butter, such as 'Lurpak' or 'President', and beat it well before adding other ingredients. The butter will lighten considerably and produce a soft, creamy white colour. Some cake bakers add titanium dioxide to their buttercream. It is considered safe to consume in the UK, although some European countries have banned its use. Another option is to use a powder called 'Superwhite' and labelled 'E171 free', which has been developed as an alternative to titanium dioxide.

AMERICAN BUTTERCREAM

American buttercream is probably the most familiar frosting. It is very easy to make and only requires two main ingredients – butter and icing sugar. It will keep in the fridge for as long as the shelf life of the butter, providing no milk has been added to soften the mixture. It freezes well, but needs to be securely wrapped as butter can easily taint by absorbing any other strong flavours that are stored nearby in the freezer. Even with just two ingredients, the results can vary enormously. This is mainly due to the type of butter used and the temperature of the ingredients.

The key to success is to ensure that real butter is used rather than a baking spread or margarine, and that it is at room temperature. It must be soft enough to leave a dent when squeezed between your thumb and finger, but not melted. As already mentioned, whether to use salted or unsalted is down to personal preference, but consider whether the buttercream will be coloured. If so, then unsalted will result in a paler buttercream that will take colour well.

American buttercream is firm, easy to pipe, and will withstand being unrefrigerated, but it will not keep in extreme heat due to its high fat content. It forms a slight crust, making it a good choice for piping more defined shapes and swirls on cakes. It does not contain eggs, which may be a consideration when preparing cakes for children or vulnerable adults. Very good plant butters are now easily available from most supermarkets, and these provide a good alternative when a dairy-free or vegan frosting is required.

The basic ratio for American buttercream is one part butter to two parts icing sugar. For example, 250g (9oz) butter and 500g (17½oz) icing sugar will be more than sufficient to pipe generous buttercream swirls on to twelve large cupcakes, or to fill and top a 20cm (8in) sandwich cake. These quantities can be adjusted depending on whether other ingredients are added. For example, when making lemon buttercream more icing sugar may be required if adding lemon juice to the mixture.

Sometimes the finished buttercream may be a little stiff, due to the butter being slightly cold or the temperature of the kitchen. If this happens, one or two teaspoons of hot water can be added to loosen the mixture. Milk is sometimes used instead of water, but this is not a good choice if the intention is to store the frosting for a few days before using it, as the keeping quality will be significantly reduced. Instead of having the 'use by' date of the butter as the shelf-life guide it will be the milk that determines how long the buttercream will keep.

American buttercream made with butter and icing sugar.

PROJECT 1: ROSE CUPCAKES

These pretty two-tone shaded cupcakes are perfect for an afternoon tea, a birthday, or to serve as individual cakes at a party or wedding buffet. This American buttercream recipe will make enough to cover twelve cupcakes.

Ingredients:

250g (9oz) unsalted butter at room temperature
500g (17½oz) icing sugar (sieved)
1tsp vanilla extract
Paste colour – dark pink and leaf green

Equipment:

Piping bag
Piping nozzles: 2D for the rose and 366 for the leaves
12 vanilla sponge cupcakes, baked in either paper cases or
    baking cups

Rose cupcakes.

Method:

Beat the butter well until it is very soft and begins to lighten. Use either a stand mixer with a beater attachment, a hand mixer, or beat by hand using a wooden spoon.

Add half the sieved icing sugar to the butter, stir slowly to begin with to avoid a 'cloud' of icing sugar, then increase the speed until it is fully incorporated. Repeat with the remaining half of the sugar.

Add the vanilla extract to the mixture and beat again. If the buttercream is very stiff, add a teaspoon or two of hot water and beat again. Repeat if necessary until the buttercream is soft and fluffy.

Remove about one third of the buttercream into a separate bowl and add a tiny amount of the pink paste colour using the end of a cocktail stick. Use a spatula to beat in the colour.

Place the 2D nozzle into the piping bag. Place the bag into a tall glass and fold down the sides of the bag. Using a small spatula, coat the inside of the bag evenly with the pink buttercream. Then fill the centre with the white buttercream.

At this stage the cupcakes can be topped with a thin coating of white buttercream before piping, or they can be left plain.

To pipe the rose swirl, hold the piping bag at a 90-degree angle above the centre of the cupcake, squeeze the bag, and make contact with the surface of the cake.

Then lift up and slowly swirl around the centre.

Keep slowly swirling around the centre again until the surface is covered. Stop squeezing and then pull the piping bag away.

Use some green-coloured buttercream and a 366 piping nozzle to pipe some leaves. These can be piped in at the pull-away point of the rose piping.

Pipe with the points of the nozzle top and bottom. Apply gentle pressure to the bag to form the leaf, and then quickly pull away to create a point on the leaf. Repeat for a second leaf.

Trouble-Shooting Tips for American Buttercream

Buttercream is hard and lumpy: This is usually due to using cold butter. The butter needs to be at room temperature, soft enough to make an indent when squeezed between your thumb and forefinger, but not melted. Add a tablespoon of hot water to the mixture and beat on a high speed until soft and fluffy.

Buttercream is grainy: This could be the result of using unsifted icing sugar. Even brands that state they are already sifted can become grainy over time due to the added anti-caking ingredients. Always sieve icing sugar before making buttercream.

Buttercream is too soft and will not hold its shape: The mixture may have become warm, so refrigerate it for ten minutes. Or insufficient icing sugar has been added to the mixture so add some more, a tablespoon at a time, until the correct consistency is achieved.

Buttercream has a lot of air bubbles in it: This is due to over beating or using a whisk instead of a beater attachment. To remove the bubbles, use a large silicone or metal spatula and spread the mixture against the side of the bowl to 'pop' the bubbles and smooth out the mixture.

SWISS MERINGUE BUTTERCREAM

This buttercream is a popular choice of frosting for professional cake decorators when making celebration and wedding cakes. It is essentially a meringue with butter added. It has a light, mousse-like consistency that takes colour and flavour well, making it a perfect choice for filling a layered cake. Although it is a relatively simple frosting to make, it does require a degree of accuracy and is time-consuming to prepare.

The egg whites and sugar are whisked together whilst being heated over a bain marie. A sugar thermometer is needed to check that the required temperature of 72°C (160°F) has been reached, and that the butter is at room temperature before being added to the meringue. Once the meringue has cooked, it is then removed from the heat and transferred to a large bowl. It needs to be continually whisked until cool and forming stiff peaks. As this can take up to 20 to 30 minutes, a stand mixer with a whisk attachment is ideal for this task, although a hand mixer can also be used.

Once the meringue is cool, the butter is then added in stages, a tablespoon at a time, using the beater attachment on the mixer. Each addition of butter needs to be fully incorporated into the meringue before the next tablespoon is added. Once all the butter has been added any flavourings can then be beaten into the mixture.

Swiss meringue buttercream can be stored at room temperature for one to two days, or refrigerated for up to five days. It will also freeze well for up to three months. If freezing, store in an airtight container, then thaw at room temperature before using.

Swiss meringue buttercream.

PROJECT 2: A 'SEMI-NAKED' CELEBRATION CAKE

This is a very popular style of celebration cake for weddings. Swiss meringue buttercream will give a light coating for either a Madeira or Victoria sponge cake. It is also a useful technique to learn, as one layer of buttercream is also known as a 'crumb coat', which forms the foundation layer for sugarpasted cakes. Crumb coating is a technique used by professional cake makers to give their cakes a smoother finish. It helps to stick down any stray crumbs before adding either another layer of buttercream or covering with sugar paste. This is known as a 'naked cake'.

A second layer of buttercream, as shown in this project, is known as 'semi-naked'. This will give a more opaque finish to the cake and offers a further opportunity to apply decorations, such as piping swirls on top or applying little shards of gold leaf to the sides.

The finish of this cake has a slightly rustic feel, so I have chosen to keep the decoration to a minimum and use pressed pansy flowers. Fresh flowers or candied fruits would also suit this style of informal celebration cake. This cake would be a perfect choice for a small, intimate summer wedding.

Ingredients:

3 × 18cm (7in) round sponge cakes baked in sandwich tins

3 large egg whites

250g (9oz) caster sugar (golden caster sugar will give a 'creamier' coloured finish)

1tsp vanilla extract or bean paste

300g (10½oz) unsalted butter

Pinch of salt (optional)

Dried flowers and gold leaf for decoration

Equipment:

Heatproof bowl

Stand mixer with beater and whisk attachment (used in this project) or hand mixer

Small hand whisk

Cake turntable

Large palette knife

Small angled spatula

Tall side scraper

Cake board/stand for presentation

'Semi-naked' celebration cake.

Method:

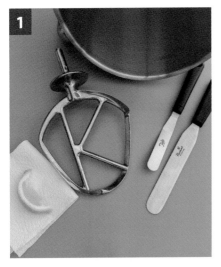

Begin by preparing all equipment to ensure it is grease free. Any fat on beaters, whisks and spoons or on the surface of mixing bowls will inhibit the egg whites from whipping. Ensure all equipment is clean and dry, and then wipe over with lemon juice.

Place the egg whites and salt (if using it) into a heatproof bowl, and place over a pan of simmering water. Ensure the base of the bowl is not in contact with the water. Whisk gently until the sugar has dissolved and the mixture no longer feels grainy when rubbed between your finger and thumb. If using a sugar thermometer, the mixture should reach a temperature of 72°C/160°F.

Remove the bowl from the heat and decant the mixture into the stand mixer bowl with the whisk attachment in place. Whisk on a medium speed until the bowl is cool and the meringue is smooth, glossy, and forming stiff peaks. This can take up to half an hour.

Once the bowl is cool, replace the whisk attachment with the beater attachment. Have the butter ready, cut into small cubes. It must be soft but not melted.

With the mixer running on a medium speed, begin to add the butter a tablespoon at a time. Each addition must be fully incorporated into the eggs before adding the next cube of butter.

Once all the butter has been incorporated, turn off the motor and add the vanilla extract. Scrape down the sides of the bowl and give the buttercream a final beat for another minute. The buttercream is now ready to use.

To fill and decorate the cakes:

Remove the cakes from the tins and level their surface if slightly domed, using either a large serrated knife or a cake leveller as shown.

Apply a small amount of buttercream to the centre of a cake board. This will secure the cake to the board. Position the first cake on the board. Use a large palette knife to top the cake with some of the buttercream. Add the second sponge and gently press down. Do not worry if the buttercream oozes out at the sides as this will be removed later.

Add buttercream to the second sponge and then top with the third sponge. If using a spirit level, check the level of the cake at this point. Place a small circle of parchment paper on the top cake and place the spirit level in the centre of the cake. Gently press the sponge until the cake is level.

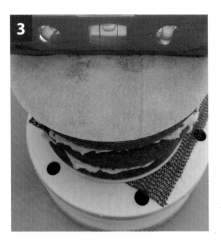

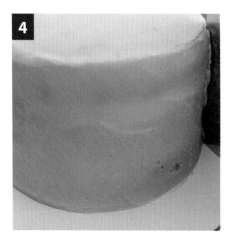

Apply buttercream to the top of the cake first and then the sides using an angled spatula. Then, using the large side scraper, sweep around the sides.

Use an angled spatula to neaten the top surface by drawing the buttercream from the outside towards the centre of the cake. Repeat until the sides and surface are smooth. The sponge will be seen through the buttercream. This layer is known as a crumb coat. Check the level again. Refrigerate the cake for fifteen minutes.

Apply a second coat of buttercream as before. The top can be swirled using a small angled spatula. Decorate with fresh or dried flowers, and add a little gold leaf to the sides for a final flourish, as shown.

Trouble-Shooting Tips for Swiss and Italian Buttercream

Meringue will not form stiff peaks: Keep whisking. The egg whites and sugar take a long time to form stiff peaks, sometimes up to 30 minutes. Unfortunately the meringue will never reach stiff peaks if there is a drop of egg yolk or grease in the mixture, mixing bowl or on any tools being used. Wipe down all the tools with lemon juice before using. If possible, avoid making this on particularly humid days where there is extra moisture in the air.

Mixer is overheating: If using a food mixer with less power, it may become overheated due to the length of time mixing. Place the attachment/beaters in the bowl with the meringue and place in the fridge for 20–30 minutes to cool everything down, and then continue whisking.

Buttercream has curdled: If the meringue has separated, curdled, or is too thick at any point after mixing in all the butter, just keep beating because it will eventually come together.

Buttercream is too thin/soupy: If the mixture has become too thin and soupy this is usually due to the butter being added whilst the meringue was still too warm. This can be easily remedied by placing the bowl and beater in the fridge for 20 minutes to cool down, then returning it to the mixer and beating on medium-high speed until it has thickened.

Buttercream has become solid in the fridge: Remove from the fridge and leave to come back up to room temperature, then place into the bowl of the stand mixer fitted with the paddle attachment and beat for two to three minutes until creamy again.

ITALIAN MERINGUE BUTTERCREAM

Italian meringue buttercream is similar in texture to Swiss meringue buttercream, but differs in that the egg whites are whisked separately from the sugar. The sugar is used as a hot sugar syrup, which is then poured on to the whisked egg whites before adding the butter. The sugar syrup produces a silky, smooth and stable buttercream. It is better able to withstand a warmer environment, which is why many professional cake makers prefer to use this buttercream when producing wedding cakes and other celebration cakes during the warmer summer months. It is also less sweet than other buttercream recipes.

Making a sugar syrup whilst whisking egg whites at the same time does require a degree of preparation, so it is a good idea to assemble all the equipment and ingredients together first and have them close to hand before starting. As this is another meringue-based buttercream, all utensils need to be completely clean and grease free, so wipe all mixing bowls and utensils with lemon juice before using.

Making a sugar syrup is not difficult, but it requires care and attention. Hot sugar syrup can cause severe burns, so take extra care when pouring the syrup on to the egg whites. A thermometer is also needed to check that the correct temperature has been reached before adding the syrup to the egg whites.

The finished Italian meringue buttercream.

PROJECT 3: ST CLEMENT'S OMBRE BIRTHDAY CAKE

This would be a suitable cake for any age group. Using hot sugar syrup effectively cooks the egg whites, which may be a dietary consideration. The ombre effect is created by using two colours of buttercream, which are then combined to create a third colour. More shades can be made combining the two base colours if a more gradual ombre effect is required. Orange and yellow colours have been used in this project and then decorated with orange and lemon sugar sprinkles. The cakes can be flavoured with the zest of the fruits and the buttercream also flavoured with a citrus extract.

St Clement's ombre birthday cake. This colourful cake would be perfect for a party.

Ingredients for Italian meringue buttercream:

3 large egg whites

200g (7oz) caster sugar

75ml water

1tsp lemon or orange extract

300g (10oz) unsalted butter

Ingredients for the cake:

1 × 18cm (7in) or 1 × 20cm (8in) round, deep sponge cake

Edible food colouring – yellow and orange (Progel paste colours have been used in this project)

Equipment:

Small saucepan

Thermometer (thermapen, or a jam or candy thermometer)

Stand mixer with the whisk attachment (used in this project) or hand mixer

Small silicone spatula

Cake turntable

Large palette knife

Small-angled spatula

Tall side scraper

Cake board/stand for presentation

Method for buttercream:

1 Begin by preparing the equipment to ensure it is grease free. The mixing bowl, beater and whisk attachment must be clean and dry; then wipe them over with lemon juice. Add the egg whites into the mixing bowl of the stand mixer with the whisk attachment.

2 Place the caster sugar and water into the small saucepan and heat gently, swirling the pan very gently to dissolve the sugar. Do not stir as sugar crystals may form. Continue heating until the temperature on the thermometer reaches 100°C/200°F.

3 Begin whisking the egg whites. The aim is to reach the stiff-peak stage at the same time as the sugar syrup reaches 120°C/250°F.

4

Once the egg whites are stiff and the sugar syrup has reached 120°C/250°F, slowly pour the syrup on to the egg whites in a steady stream with the motor running on its lowest speed. Try to avoid pouring on to the whisk attachment: aim for the space between the whisk and the side of the bowl.

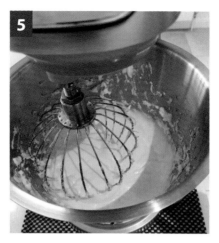

5

Keep the mixer running on its lowest speed until all the syrup has been added, and then turn it up to medium speed and continue whisking until the bowl has cooled down to room temperature. Have the butter ready, cut into small cubes. It must be soft but not melted.

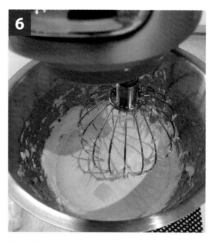

6

With the mixer running on a medium speed, begin to add the butter a cube at a time. Each addition must be fully incorporated into the meringue mixture before adding the next tablespoon of butter.

7

Once all the butter has been incorporated turn off the motor and add the lemon extract. Scrape down the sides of the bowl, then give the buttercream a final beat for another minute. The buttercream is now ready to use. Fill and crumb coat following the instructions in the previous project. Refrigerate for fifteen to twenty minutes to firm it up.

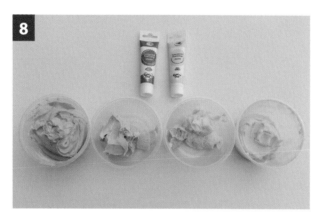

8

Take four bowls. Decant the buttercream into two of the bowls. Colour one with yellow paste and the other with the orange paste colour. Add the colour with the tip of a cocktail stick to avoid adding too much. To make the two remaining shades, scoop some of the orange buttercream and a small amount of yellow into the third bowl and mix well. In the fourth bowl mix a scoop of the lemon colour with a small amount of the orange. The colours are now ready to use.

9

Set the cake on to a turntable. Measure the height of the cake and roughly divide by four. Use a palette knife to mark the side of the cake into four bands. This will act as a rough guide when applying the bands of colours. Using a large palette knife, apply the orange shade of buttercream to the bottom band of the cake.

How to decorate the ombre cake:

This can be done by using two colours and combining the two to create a third colour. Or one colour can be used and then have two lighter shades added, so the colour is darkest at the base and becomes gradually lighter.

In this project I am using two strong colours for the top and bottom of the cake and then combining these colours to create two further colours, which will create the 'ombre' effect of two colours merging into each other.

Clean the palette knife and apply the second band of buttercream. This colour will be the mix of orange/yellow.

Clean the palette knife again and apply the third band of yellow/orange buttercream.

For the top of the cake and the top band apply the yellow buttercream to the top of the cake first, and then use the palette knife to bring the buttercream over the edge to coat the top band of colour.

Use the large side scraper to gently scrape round the sides with a sweeping action. Ensure the scraper is upright and brought towards you at an angle of about 45 degrees. Eventually the colours will merge and the icing will be smooth.

Use the scraper or angled spatula to neaten the top surface by drawing the buttercream from the outside edge towards the centre of the cake. Place the cake back into the fridge for fifteen minutes to set.

Without mixing the colours together, place the remaining buttercream into a piping bag fitted with a large piping nozzle. Pipe swirls on the top of the cake. Finish with some edible sprinkles.

OTHER TYPES OF BUTTERCREAM FROSTINGS

French Buttercream

French buttercream is made in the same way as Italian buttercream, but uses egg yolks instead of whites. It has a rich, buttery flavour and creamy texture and is yellow in colour due to the egg yolks. It is important to use only pasteurised eggs as the yolks may not be fully cooked using this process.

Like Italian meringue, it is a more difficult buttercream to master as it also relies on accuracy. The temperature of the sugar syrup must reach the soft ball stage (115°C/237°F) before being poured on to the whisked egg yolks. This mixture then needs to be cool, before adding the soft butter in stages.

This buttercream has a soft consistency so is mostly used for fillings such as macarons, small cake toppings and as a base for fruit tarts instead of crème patisserie. When colouring, it can be difficult to get an accurate lighter shade due to having a yellow base colour. However, it does take flavours well, which can be added to the finished buttercream. Cooled, melted chocolate added to the buttercream will make a delicious, easy-to-spread covering for a chocolate cake. This buttercream can also be piped on to small cupcakes or as an embellishment for larger cakes.

The buttercream can be stored in the fridge for up to three days or in the freezer for up to three months.

German Buttercream

This buttercream is also known as crème mousseline or custard buttercream. It can be used as a filling and coating, or can be piped. As one of its names suggests, this buttercream is made by using a custard base. It uses whole eggs, so the finished buttercream has a pale yellow colour. It has a rich, custard-like flavour, reminiscent of ice cream. It is an easier buttercream to make than the meringue-based buttercreams as it does not require accurate measuring or specialist equipment.

The custard base is made using whole eggs, sugar, cornflour and milk. The custard is then allowed to cool to room temperature, before being added in stages to softened, whipped butter. The custard base can also be made ahead of time, covered and stored overnight.

Flavourings such as vanilla seeds, vanilla bean paste or extract, instant coffee granules or extract, fruit powders or cocoa powder can be incorporated into the buttercream either by adding to the milk before cooking, or mixing into the finished buttercream. Flavours such as lemon curd, salted caramel and cooled melted chocolate can also be folded into the finished buttercream, but this will change the consistency to a softer mixture. To colour the buttercream, use either paste or powder colours folded into the finished buttercream.

German buttercream can be stored in the fridge for up to three days or in the freezer for up to three months.

This buttercream would be a perfect choice for piping on cakes that have a slightly tangier or sharper flavour, such as those containing summer berries, raspberries or gooseberries. The creamy, custard-like flavour works particularly well with cakes containing rhubarb.

Ermine Buttercream

This buttercream is also known as flour buttercream. It is made by making a roux base of flour, sugar and milk. Once cold, the flour mixture is then incorporated into whisked, soft, unsalted butter. The result has a light, mousse-like consistency. It has an almost 'cream cheese' mouth feel, even though it does not contain any cheese. This makes it a very good alternative to cakes that usually have a cream cheese frosting such as carrot cake or red velvet cake.

Flavourings and colourings, described above, can be incorporated in exactly the same way as German buttercream.

The flour base for the buttercream can be prepared ahead of time and stored in the fridge overnight. The finished buttercream will keep in the fridge for up to a week, or can be frozen in a sealed container for up to three months. As with all stored buttercreams, it will need to come back up to room temperature and be re-beaten before using.

Russian Buttercream

Russian buttercream is a lesser known buttercream, which is becoming increasingly popular due to its simplicity to make. It has only two main ingredients – butter and sweetened condensed milk. It is made in a similar way to American buttercream, which begins by beating softened, unsalted butter for at least five minutes until very soft, white and fluffy. Then, instead of adding icing sugar, condensed milk is beaten into the butter in stages. The buttercream is smooth and has a similar texture to thick whipped cream.

As well as being easy to make, it is easily rescued if it begins to split and looks sloppy. This is usually caused by the butter being too warm. Simply place the buttercream, still in its mixing bowl along with the beater, into the fridge for fifteen minutes, and then remove and re-beat until light and fluffy again.

Flavour extracts such as vanilla, coffee and fruit as well as cocoa and espresso powder can be added to the beaten butter before adding the condensed milk. To add colour, paste colours and powders can be folded into the finished buttercream. An alternative to using ordinary sweetened condensed milk is 'Dulce de Lèche', or caramel condensed milk. This, combined with a pinch of sea-salt flakes, will create a delicious salted caramel buttercream, perfect for covering a toffee or chocolate cake.

This buttercream is best used on the day it is made as bubbles begin to form if it is left for a long period of time. Using a silicone spatula to fold the mixture through will help to eliminate some of the bubbles and create a smoother buttercream.

Cream Cheese Buttercream

Cream cheese buttercream, usually known as frosting, is a popular cake covering and filling for spiced cakes such as carrot cake, passion cake and red velvet, which use oil in the recipe rather than butter or baking spread. It is made with a mixture of butter, sugar and cream cheese. As it contains a high quantity of cream cheese, any cakes covered or filled with it must be refrigerated, so choose a cake recipe that uses oil rather than butter as the sponge is less likely to dry out when stored in the fridge.

Full-fat cream cheese is required as low-fat cheese contains too much water and will result in a sloppy mixture that unfortunately cannot be rectified. Equal quantities of unsalted butter and icing sugar and a double quantity of cream cheese are required: for example 125g (4½oz) of butter, 125g of icing sugar and 250g (9oz) of cream cheese. Drain off any liquid in the cream cheese container before weighing.

To make the frosting, beat the soft butter and icing sugar together until light and fluffy before adding the cream cheese. If using a stand mixer or hand mixer, this mixture will combine and become thick and smooth after a few minutes. If mixing by hand, it will take at least five to six minutes. Vanilla bean paste or extract can be added to the finished mixture. Orange or lemon zest also makes a delicious flavouring, and this can be incorporated when beating the cream cheese into the butter and sugar mixture. Cooled, melted white chocolate can also be added to cream-cheese frosting. Although this produces a firmer frosting when cold and pipes well, it still needs to be refrigerated due to the buttercream's high fat content.

How to Make Rolled Buttercream

Sugarpaste is still one of the most popular cake coverings for wedding and other celebration cakes, but over the last few years the trend for buttercream-covered cakes has seen a rise in popularity. Recipes have recently been developed that incorporate the look of smooth fondant, but with the flavour and texture of buttercream. Rolled buttercream, as the name suggests, can be rolled out to cover cakes, as well as being firm enough to use in moulds and to model small decorations. The original recipe was developed in the USA and uses light corn syrup. Corn syrup is not readily available to buy in the UK, so a combination of liquid glucose and golden syrup can be used instead. The resulting texture is the same, but the colour will be a pale golden shade, with a slightly 'toffee' flavour.

Ingredients:
125g (4½oz) butter
125ml corn syrup (or use 90g (3oz) liquid glucose and 35g (1oz) golden syrup)
500g (17½oz) icing sugar (plus roughly 300–500g (10–17½oz) extra for kneading)

Method:
1. Beat the butter for ten minutes until soft, creamy and pale.
2. Slowly add in syrup.
3. Using a spatula, add 500g (17½oz) of icing sugar until mostly incorporated.
4. Dust the work surface liberally with the extra icing sugar, before turning out the paste on to it.
5. Add more icing sugar and knead the buttercream until a smooth dough forms.
6. Continue incorporating the extra icing sugar until it no longer feels sticky and the excess icing sugar stops being absorbed.
7. The finished paste will feel smooth.
8. Refrigerate for twenty minutes to firm up a little. It can then be coloured, by kneading in a little paste colour, before rolling out.
9. This paste can be used to top cupcakes, with moulds, or even to top and coat the sides of larger cakes. It is quite a fragile paste, so if using it to coat the sides of a cake, roll it out on to an acetate strip to support it when positioning it around the cake.

CHAPTER 4

MARZIPAN

· · · · · · · · ·

Marzipan is a sweet dough made using ground almonds and sugar. It is traditionally used as a cake covering for rich fruit celebration cakes such as Christmas cake and wedding cakes, as well as a covering and filling for other cakes such as simnel cake, which is served at Easter. In the UK, marzipan and almond paste are the same, but in other countries they are often sold as different products. By using different ratios of sugar and almonds, the paste has a different texture and consistency.

Its origins are unclear, but many food historians believe the confection came originally from the Middle East and was then introduced into Europe in the late Middle Ages. In England, various recipes for marzipan have been traced as far back as the fifteenth century. It was known as 'marchpane', and rather than using the paste as a covering or

A selection of fruits modelled from marzipan.

filling, it was used to sculpt decorative plaques, figures and other objects such as models of buildings. These became ornaments at large banquets and feasts. The paste was much firmer and was used as a decoration rather than as an edible sweet.

Various recipes for marzipan can be found across the world. In the southern European countries of Spain (notably in Toledo), Portugal, Greece, southern Italy and Malta, marzipan is often used to make sweets and treats for seasonal and religious celebrations as well as birthdays and weddings.

The marzipan is often shaped and coloured to represent fruits or animals as well as being coated in chocolate. It is also used as a filling for pastries and biscuits.

In the Netherlands, Belgium, Luxembourg and northern France, marzipan figures are gifted to celebrate Saint Nicholas Day on 6 December.

Germany is regarded by many as the centre of marzipan manufacturing, particularly in the city of Lübeck. Manufacturers such as Niederegger pride themselves on producing a marzipan of the highest quality by guaranteeing that their marzipan contains two-thirds of almonds by weight. Marzipan sweets, shaped as a loaf of bread (Marzipanbrot) and small potatoes (Marzipankartoffeln) are sold across Germany, as well as being exported over the Christmas season. Another popular Christmas treat is Stollen, which is an enriched fruit bread with a marzipan centre. A traditional New Year gift is a marzipan pig known as a 'lucky pig' (Glücksschwein).

'Mozartkugel' from Austria are another popular confection at Christmas time. These sweets are made by combining marzipan with pistachio and nougat, moulded into a ball and then dipped into dark chocolate.

In northern Europe, Denmark, Sweden and Norway Christmas and New Year are also celebrated with treats of marzipan pigs, and at Eastertime, marzipan is shaped into eggs. Marzipan is also a popular ingredient for cakes, such as 'Kransekage', as well as fillings for pastries, such as Danish pastries. The traditional Swedish cake known as

'Prinsesstårta', or princess cake, is a dome-shaped, cream-filled sponge covered with a light green coloured marzipan. It is often decorated with a pink marzipan rose.

A traditional New Year gift is a marzipan pig, thought to bring good luck.

Persipan

Some cheaper marzipan sold in supermarkets is actually persipan. This is a very similar paste to marzipan, but is made using apricot or peach kernels instead of almonds. It is often used as a substitute filling in commercial cakes and biscuits as it is considerably cheaper to make. To counteract the bitter taste of the fruit kernels, persipan contains more sugar than marzipan.

PROJECT 4: TWO WAYS TO COVER A FRUIT CAKE BEFORE ICING

The traditional method for covering a rich fruit cake is to cover the cake with a layer of marzipan before adding a top coat of icing. It gives a smooth base for the icing as well as providing a barrier to stop any jam or sugar syrup seeping through into the top layer of icing and spoiling the final decoration. It provides an airtight covering, which extends the shelf life of the cake.

There are two methods for applying the marzipan, and the method used is dependent on which icing is used for the final covering – sugarpaste or royal icing. Sugarpaste (also known as fondant icing, rolled icing or 'ready-to-roll' icing) is a stiff, sweet dough that is rolled out using a rolling pin. It is a quick and easy covering to apply.

Royal icing is the traditional coating to use on a marzipan-covered cake. It is applied with a palette knife and requires two or three coatings of icing to give a smooth, opaque finish. This is known as flat icing. A quicker and easier method is to apply one coat of royal icing thickly in swirls, as shown in Project 14 in Chapter 7.

Good quality, ready-made marzipan can be found in most supermarkets. It has a soft, pliable consistency once kneaded, and is available to buy as white or yellow (golden) marzipan. White marzipan is the better option for cake covering as the yellow has added food colouring that may show through the top coat of icing and spoil the appearance of the finished cake. Raw sugar marzipan is available to buy in most health food shops or online retailers. It is dark in colour due to the dark colour of the sugar in the recipe and, again, is not suitable for covering cakes.

HOW TO MAKE MARZIPAN

Marzipan is easy to make at home, although it is not a more cost-effective option. Care needs to be taken not to overknead the paste, as this will cause the almond oils to leach, which may discolour and spoil the icing. This quick and easy recipe will make 500g (17½oz) of marzipan.

Ingredients:

250g (9oz) ground almonds
125g (4½oz) caster sugar
125g (4½oz) icing sugar
1tsp lemon juice
½tsp almond extract
1 large egg white

Method:

Mix the ground almonds and both sugars together in a bowl. Make a well in the centre and add the lemon juice, almond extract and most of the egg white. Mix to a firm but soft dough, adding more of the egg white if necessary. Lightly knead on a work surface dusted with icing sugar until any cracks have disappeared and the paste is smooth. Wrap in clingfilm or waxed paper until ready to use.

Two ways to cover a fruit cake with marzipan ready for icing.

When covering a cake with homemade marzipan, allow the paste to dry out for a day or two before covering with icing.

Quantity of Marzipan Required for Different Cake Sizes, with a Depth of 7.5cm (3in)

This guide can also be used for sugarpaste quantities.

Cake Size	Round	Square
15cm/6in	500g/17½oz	750g/26½oz
17cm/6.7in	750g/26½oz	875g/31oz
20cm/8in	875g/31oz	1kg/2lb
22cm/8.7in	1kg/2lb	1.25kg/3lb
25cm/9.8in	1.25kg/3lb	1.5kg/3½lb
27cm/10.6in	1.5kg/3½lb	1.75kg/4lb
30cm/11.8in	1.75kg/4lb	2.2kg/5lb

ALL-IN-ONE METHOD

This is the easiest way to cover a cake with marzipan. It produces a finish with rounded edges and corners, so is best used for cakes that are to be covered with sugarpaste or swirled royal icing.

Ingredients:

Fruit or Madeira cake
Marzipan
Apricot glaze
Icing sugar

Equipment:

Cake board or drum
Rolling pin
Icing sugar sifter
Cake smoother (ideally two)
Pastry brush or small angled spatula
Large sharp knife
Pizza wheel (optional)
Tape measure and/or string

Before beginning either of the methods shown, calculate the quantity of marzipan required for the size and shape of the cake (*see* box above). As a general rule, the depth of marzipan and sugarpaste when rolled out is 5mm (0.02in), but this can vary according to both preference and the brand of paste used. Guides, such as spacers or guide rings attached to the rolling pin, will help roll the marzipan to the correct thickness.

Begin by trimming the top of the cake with either a large serrated knife or a cake wire if it has a very domed top. If the cake has only a slightly domed surface leave it as it is, as this will be rectified later when applying the marzipan.

Measure the cake's depth (on the opposite sides of the cake) and diameter to give an approximate measurement for your rolled-out marzipan. For example, a 15cm (6in) cake with a depth of 7.5cm (3in) will be 15cm + 7.5cm + 7.5cm= 30cm (12in). The approximate diameter of the rolled-out marzipan will be 30cm. Place the cake upside down on to the cake board or drum.

3 Make the apricot glaze. Warm some apricot jam with a splash of water in either a pan or a microwave, and heat until bubbling. Remove from the heat and sieve the jam. Set aside to cool.

4 Brush the surface and sides of the cake with the apricot glaze as well as the top edge.

5 Plug any holes in the cake surface with some small pieces of marzipan. Roll out a thin sausage of marzipan and use this to fill the gap between the cake and the board.

Dust the work surface with icing sugar (do not use cornflour), and knead the marzipan until it is soft and pliable. Begin rolling, remembering to lift and turn frequently until the depth of the paste is 5mm (0.2in). A helpful guide is to use ring guides on the rolling pin (as shown) or spacers.

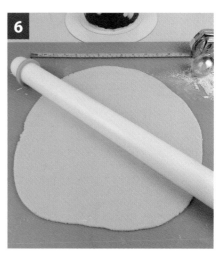

6

7 Use the rolling pin to help lift and lower the marzipan over the cake. Smooth the top of the cake first with your hands, and then use a cake smoother. When covering a square cake, press the corners into the cake first before smoothing down the sides.

8 Smooth the sides by lifting the paste away from the cake with one hand and smooth down the paste with the other hand. This is done to avoid any folds or creases forming in the paste. Finish by smoothing the sides with a cake smoother. Ideally have another smoother in the opposite hand to prevent making finger marks.

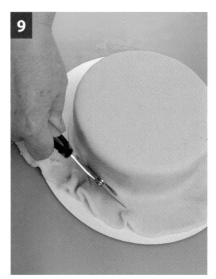

9 Trim the excess paste away with either a sharp knife or with a pizza wheel, as shown here. If commercial marzipan has been used the cake can be iced straightaway. If using homemade marzipan, then allow the paste to dry out for at least 24 hours before icing.

PANEL METHOD

When preparing a cake to flat ice with royal icing, the cake will need a flat top, straight sides and sharp edges. Sugarpasted cakes with sharp edges are extremely popular, and this method for attaching marzipan should be used to achieve this finish. The marzipan is attached in two parts for a round or oval cake, first the top and then the sides. For a square, hexagonal or octagonal cake, each side has separate panels of marzipan applied, which is why it is known as the 'panel' method.

The ingredients and equipment needed are the same as the all-in-one method described previously. Measure the diameter, depth and circumference of the cake, and prepare it as in the all-in-one method by plugging any holes in the cake surface and glazing with apricot glaze.

Method for covering a round or oval cake:

Brush the top of the cake with some apricot glaze, then dust the work surface with icing sugar. Use two thirds of the marzipan and knead until soft and pliable. Remember to lift and turn frequently to avoid the paste sticking to the work surface. Roll out the paste until the diameter is slightly larger than the diameter of the top of the cake, and the depth is 5mm (0.2in).

Place the disc of marzipan on to a sheet of baking paper, lightly dusted with icing sugar. Then place the cake upside down on to the marzipan disc, so that the glazed surface is in contact with the marzipan.

Trim the excess paste to within 1cm (0.4in) of the cake. Use a small palette knife to press the excess marzipan into the sides so it becomes level with the sides of the cake.

Turn the cake the right way up and place it back on to the cake board or drum. Remove the baking paper and brush the sides with apricot glaze.

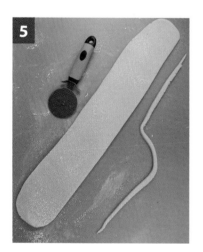

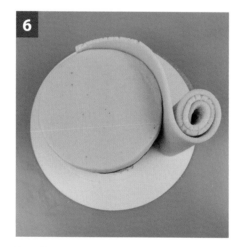

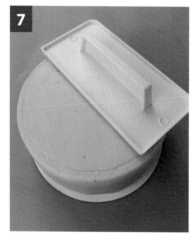

Knead the remaining marzipan and then roll out a long strip measuring slightly more than the length and width of the circumference and height of the cake. Trim one long side of the strip to give one straight edge.

Dust the marzipan strip very lightly with icing sugar and roll it up loosely like a bandage. Place the cut edge of the roll on to the board and then unroll it around the cake.

Use a small palette knife to trim away the excess paste around the top, and smooth the joins together so the surface is level and even. Finally, use a cake smoother around the sides and top to give a neat finish.

Method for covering a square, hexagonal or octagonal cake:

1. Follow the instructions above to prepare the cake and cover the top.
2. Measure the length and depth of each side of the cake. Instead of rolling out one long strip for the circumference of the cake as when covering a round cake, each side will need a panel of marzipan cut to the size of the side measurement.
3. Brush the sides of the cake with apricot glaze before attaching the panels to the sides of the cake.
4. Use a small palette knife to trim away the excess paste around the top and smooth the joins together so the surface is level and even. Finally, use a cake smoother around the sides and top, but avoid smoothing the corners.

PROJECT 5: BATTENBERG CAKE

A Battenberg cake.

A Battenberg is a traditional English cake. It is sometimes known as 'window cake' or 'chapel window cake' due to its chequerboard appearance resembling windows. It is believed to have been created to celebrate the 1884 wedding of Prince Louis of Battenburg to Queen Victoria's granddaughter Princess Victoria. The cake became popular to buy when large commercial bakeries such as Lyons began producing them on an industrial scale during the 1950s. Today, television shows such as *The Great British Bake Off* have revived interest in this recipe as a home-baked treat. The following recipe has been adapted from one provided by Silverwood, who manufacture the Battenberg tin.

Ingredients:

175g (6oz) soft butter
175g (6oz) golden caster sugar
175g (6oz) self-raising flour
½tsp baking powder
50g (2oz) ground almonds
3 eggs (beaten)
Pink colouring (Progel concentrated food colour)
½tsp almond extract
½tsp vanilla extract
3tbsp apricot jam (sieved)
500g (17½oz) marzipan

Equipment:

Battenberg tin (Silverwood or Tala)
Alternatively, use a 20cm (8in) square baking tin
Take a 30 × 20cm (12 × 8in) strip of baking parchment and make an 8cm (3in) fold in the centre. This will create a division in the cake so that the two differently coloured sponges can be cooked at the same time.

Method for the sponges:

1. Pre-heat the oven to 180°C/160°C fan/gas mark 4. Assemble, grease and flour the Battenberg tin.
2. Beat together the butter and sugar until light and creamy, then gradually add the beaten eggs, before folding in the flour, baking powder and ground almonds.
3. Divide the mixture equally into two bowls. Put a few drops of pink food colouring into one half of the mixture, add ½tsp vanilla extract and mix gently until fully incorporated. Add ½tsp almond extract into the other bowl.
4. Place in the centre of the oven and bake for approximately 25 minutes, or until evenly coloured and firm to the touch. Allow the cake to cool in the tin.

Decorating the cake:

This cake will keep in an airtight container for up to a week or frozen for up to three months.

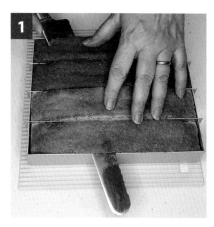

If the cake has risen above the top of the tin, use a serrated knife to cut across the top to remove the excess cake.

When completely cold, brush the apricot jam on to the long sides of the cakes and join one plain and one pink slice together and then one pink and one plain on top, creating a chequered pattern. Brush the apricot jam over all the long sides.

Roll out the marzipan on to some baking parchment dusted with icing sugar, making a rectangle approximately 20 × 30cm (8 × 12in). Place the cake on to the marzipan so that one edge is lined up to the edge of the marzipan. Completely wrap the marzipan around the cake. Trim away any surplus marzipan and both ends of the cake with a clean knife to neaten the appearance.

Colour some of the offcuts of marzipan with the pink food colouring, and use to cut out some flowers using a plunger cutter.

Use some of the uncoloured paste to create the leaves using a leaf plunger cutter. Brush with a little hot water to stick the flowers on to the cake.

COLOURING MARZIPAN

Marzipan takes colour well. Knead the marzipan until soft and workable before adding either paste colours or edible dust colours. Be aware that the end result will differ to the paste or dust colour as the marzipan is a natural beige rather than white.

It is possible to whiten marzipan, before adding other colours. The original whitener used in the confectionary business is titanium dioxide, also known as E171. It is largely considered safe to consume, although many countries around the world have banned its use. Its use in the UK is currently under review, so now manufacturers have developed an alternative and reformulated the product. It is called 'Superwhite' and labelled 'E171 free'. It is available to buy online or from specialist cake-decorating shops. For 500g marzipan, you need approximately three teaspoons of the white powder. Knead the marzipan until it is soft, add one teaspoon of powder and knead again. Continue adding and kneading until all the powder is incorporated and the marzipan has turned white.

For a chocolate and orange Battenberg, use orange zest or extract to colour one half of the sponge and cocoa powder for the other.

Chocolate marzipan can also easily be made by kneading cocoa powder into the marzipan. Warming the marzipan for five seconds in a microwave will make the paste softer and more malleable when adding the cocoa.

Colouring marzipan.

Whitening marzipan before colouring will give brighter colours.

PROJECT 6: PRINSESSTÅRTA CAKE

Swedish Princess Cake or Prinsesstårta is a popular celebration cake in Sweden.

This is a popular celebration cake from Sweden. The recipe was created in 1948 by Jenny Åkerström, who was a home economist as well as a teacher of the three daughters of Prince Carl, Duke of Västergötland. It was originally known as Grön Tårta (green cake), but was given the name Prinsesstårta as it was believed to be a favourite cake of the princesses.

The cake is a rich Genoese sponge filled with raspberry jam, patisserie cream and a large quantity of thick whipped cream, and covered with light green-coloured marzipan. The traditional decoration is a pink rose, which is also made from coloured marzipan. The following recipe has been adapted from the original recipe by Mary Berry.

Ingredients for the patisserie cream:
600ml (20fl oz) whole milk
1 vanilla pod split in half lengthways and seeds scraped out
6 egg yolks
100g (3½oz) caster sugar
50g (2oz) cornflour
50g (2oz) unsalted butter

Ingredients for the cake layers:
4 large eggs
150g (5½oz) caster sugar
1tsp vanilla extract
150g (5½oz) self-raising flour
50g (2oz) butter, melted

Other ingredients:

700g (25oz) marzipan – colour 600g (21oz) with green food-colouring paste and 100g (3½oz) with pink food-colouring paste

100g (3½oz) raspberry jam

600ml (20fl oz) double cream

Equipment:

3 × 20cm (8in) sandwich-cake tins

Baking paper for cake-tin liners

Whisk, either a stand mixer with a whisk attachment or a hand whisk

Angled spatula

Silicone spatula or large metal spoon

Wire cooling rack

25cm (10in) cake board or cake drum

Plunger leaf cutter (optional)

Icing sugar

Method for the patisserie cream:

1. In a saucepan, heat the milk gently with the vanilla seeds and pod.
2. In a large bowl, whisk the eggs, sugar and cornflour together.

Patisserie cream can be made in advance and stored in the fridge for up to two days.

3. When the milk reaches just boiling point, take it off the heat, remove the vanilla pod and pour on to the egg mixture, whisking continuously.
4. Pour the mixture back into the pan and slowly bring to the boil whilst continuing to whisk as the mixture thickens.
5. Remove from the heat and add the butter, whisking until melted and fully incorporated into the mixture
6. Transfer to a bowl and leave to cool and set for several hours in the fridge. To avoid a 'skin' forming on top, place clingfilm straight on to the cream, covering the entire surface.

Method for the sponge cakes:

1. Use three 20cm (8in) shallow sandwich tins. Alternatively, one deep cake tin can be used and the cake cut into three layers. Preheat the oven to 180°C/160°C fan/gas mark 4.
2. Grease the sides and bottom of the tins, then line the bases of the tins with baking parchment.
3. Put the eggs, sugar and vanilla extract into a large bowl and whisk together until the mixture is very pale, foamy and thick.
4. Next add the sifted flour. Using a figure-of-eight movement, gently fold in the flour using either a large metal spoon or silicone spatula.
5. Pour the cooled, melted butter down the side of the bowl and gently fold into the mixture until fully incorporated.

Three sandwich cakes, ready to assemble.

6. Divide the mixture evenly between the three tins. Bake in the preheated oven for 8–10 minutes (25–30 minutes for one deep cake) until a golden-brown colour and springy to the touch.

7. Remove from the oven and set aside to cool in the tins. When cool enough to handle, turn out on to a wire rack and remove the baking paper liners.

Assembling the cake:

1. Remove the patisserie cream from the fridge and slightly beat it if it has become very stiff. Whip the double cream until forming stiff peaks. The raspberry jam needs to be at room temperature.

2. Place the first cake layer on to the cake board. Spread a thin layer of raspberry jam on top, avoiding the edges of the cake. Then spread a generous layer of patisserie cream over the jam.

3. Add the second cake layer and repeat with a layer of jam and then patisserie cream.

4. Place the final cake layer on top and spoon on the whipped cream.

5. Knead the marzipan until smooth and pliable. Colour 600g (21oz) of the marzipan pale green and the remainder pink. Cover the green marzipan and set aside.

Begin by having all the components of the cake ready.

Use an angled spatula to smooth the cream into a small dome shape on top of the cake and thinly cover the sides. Place in the fridge for an hour.

Measure the width and the depth of the cake before rolling out the green marzipan.

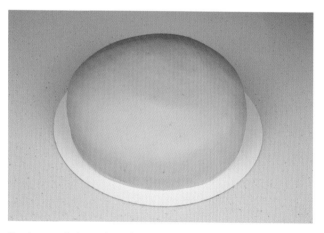

Gently smooth the surface of the cake with your hands. Avoid using too much pressure.

To make the marzipan roses:

Begin by rolling seven small balls of pink marzipan, one the size of a hazelnut and the remaining six balls the size of chickpeas. Take the largest ball and roll into a cone shape.

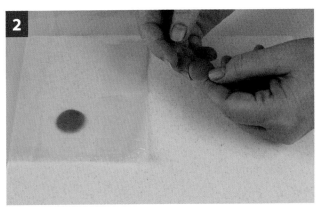

To make the petals, take the remaining balls of paste and pinch each ball between finger and thumb to form a petal shape. Squeeze outwards to thin the edge of the petal. The petal can be made even finer by placing it between a clear plastic sheet and pushing outwards nearly all the way round the edge (leave part of the edge a little thicker).

Wrap one petal round the cone, with the thicker edge at the bottom, so that it covers the cone as shown.

Take two more petals and attach them to the cone opposite each other, overlapping on one side and tucking in on the other side as shown. Stop at this stage if making a bud. Finally attach the remaining three petals by overlapping them around the cone as shown to create the full rose.

To complete the flowers, squeeze the base between your fingers, and twist to remove the excess paste. Alternatively, cut the base away using a small knife. Make an assortment of roses and buds.

To make rose leaves, use some of the green marzipan and add a little more food colouring to make a darker shade. Roll out thinly on a work surface lightly dusted with icing sugar. Cut out some leaves using a plunger cutter, or use a small knife to cut out some leaf shapes. Set aside to dry out.

Final decoration of the cake:

1. Dust the work surface lightly with icing sugar and roll out the green marzipan to a 40cm (15.7in) diameter circle, large enough to cover the cake.

2. Remove the cake from the fridge and check the measurement of the cake, before lifting the marzipan up over the cake. Use your hands to gently smooth and shape the marzipan around the sides and over the top for a smooth finish. Trim away the excess paste around the bottom of the cake.

3. Roll some of the remaining green marzipan into two long thin sausages. Twist together to create a rope. Use this to decorate the base of the cake. Attach with warm water using a small brush. Alternatively, use a ribbon to decorate the base.

Finally, dab a little warm water on the top of the cake to attach the roses and leaves. The cake can be stored in the fridge for up to two days, but is best served on the day it is made.

CHAPTER 5

CHOCOLATE

· · · · · · · · · · ·

Chocolate is probably one of everybody's favourite treats, and most people have a favourite type and brand. It is a popular food product in cake making, both as an ingredient in cakes as well as being used for cake decoration. It also has the added advantage of having a long shelf life if stored correctly. Unopened chocolate bars in sealed packaging and cocoa powder will keep for at least a year, if not longer.

A BRIEF HISTORY OF CHOCOLATE

Chocolate is manufactured from cocoa beans. These beans, found inside the cacao pods, are grown on cacao trees in hot climates across the world such as Central and South America, although 70 per cent of the world's cocoa beans are now grown in West Africa.

In 1528, Christopher Colombus and his son Ferdinand brought cocoa beans from Mexico to Spain. Chocolate was first introduced to Britain as a medicine for curing common ailments by Spanish merchants, seeking to trade with Queen Elizabeth I. There is documented evidence of drinking chocolate a century later, but it was still regarded as an expensive, rare ingredient, so was only available to the wealthy.

During the seventeenth century, drinking chocolate increased in popularity among the royal courts and aristocracy in Europe. The bitter taste of the raw chocolate was sweetened with sugar, vanilla and ground almonds.

In 1828, a Dutch chemist called Coenraad van Houten invented a press to extract the cocoa butter from the nibs. This significantly reduced the cocoa fat content, leaving behind a dense cake of cocoa powder. He also found that

'From Bean to Bar': this cake topper plaque was made using sugarpaste and modelling chocolate. It depicts the process of making chocolate from cacao pod to chocolate bar.

when alkaline salts were added to cocoa powder, the cocoa became richer, deeper in colour and easier to dissolve in water or milk. This is the origin of the term known as 'Dutch-processed cocoa' that is still used today. This cocoa powder was more palatable to drink and could be produced on a larger scale, making it much more affordable.

In the 1830s, Joseph Cadbury bought a Van Houten press for his factory in Birmingham. In 1847, another English chocolate maker called Joseph Storrs Fry also bought a press and went on to develop the chocolate bar. In 1873, Fry created the first chocolate Easter egg.

The manufacture and development of chocolate and its flavouring became extremely competitive, and continues to be so today.

HOW COCOA AND CHOCOLATE ARE MANUFACTURED

In the first stage of manufacturing chocolate the cocoa beans are harvested, allowed to ferment and then dried. They are then sorted to remove any damaged ones, before being put into sacks and exported to chocolate manufacturers.

Once the beans arrive at the manufacturer, they are cleaned and then roasted. This process gives the beans their distinctive taste and colour. As the beans roast, machines are used to crack the beans open, separating and removing the outer husks from the cocoa nibs inside. This process is called winnowing. Ground, roasted cocoa nibs are used as cocoa powder.

The next step in the chocolate-making process is to grind the nibs to a paste, called cocoa mass: this contains equal quantities of cocoa solids and cocoa butter. At this point the cocoa is dark and very bitter.

The next step in the process is called conching. This technique was developed by Rodolphe Lindt, a Swiss chocolatier, in the late nineteenth century. The cocoa mass is ground further through large rollers to produce a smooth mixture. Sugar and other flavourings are then added. Milk is also added at this stage when making milk chocolate.

The paste is then blended with more cocoa butter. The amount added depends on the type of chocolate being made. The more cocoa butter that is added, the paler the colour of the finished chocolate. Dark chocolate contains the least amount.

The final stage in the chocolate-making process is tempering. This involves heating and cooling the paste to break down crystals that have formed in the cocoa butter. It results in the chocolate having a smooth, even texture and a deep shine.

DIFFERENT TYPES OF CHOCOLATE AND THEIR PERCENTAGES

When choosing chocolate to use for a cake covering or decoration, it is useful to have a basic understanding of the different types available, and which will best suit the purpose. There are four main types of chocolate: dark, milk, white and ruby. Within these four main types are other chocolates with different percentages of cocoa. The cocoa percentage simply means the amount of cocoa the manufacturer has used in the bar of chocolate. Percentage ratings vary in different countries, but in general terms, the higher the percentage, the stronger the flavour and the darker the colour. Most chocolate is available to buy as blocks, chips or callets.

Dark Chocolate

Dark chocolate is the best to use in baking as it has a deeper flavour. Most recipes for rich chocolate coatings ask for chocolate with a percentage of 70 per cent or above, which has a stronger cocoa content, with a more bitter taste. This may be needed if other ingredients, such as caramel, are to be added to the recipe. Dark chocolate takes flavourings well, such as citrus zest or freeze-dried fruit powders. Using dark chocolate with a percentage of 50 per cent works well for buttercreams and ganache. It still has a rich flavour but without the bitterness, which many find more palatable.

Only oil-based or powdered flavourings and colourings can be added to chocolate, as water-based ones will not blend and cause the chocolate to 'seize' (this means the chocolate will separate and turn hard and lumpy).

> ## Varieties of Chocolate
>
> **Cacao nibs and powder**: This is the raw, unroasted cacao seed.
> **Cocoa nibs and cocoa powder**: Cocoa is the roasted equivalent to cacao.
> **Dutch-processed cocoa powder**: This is alkalised cocoa powder, which has a more neutral pH, is redder in colour and is less bitter than regular cocoa powder.
> **Dark chocolate**: Made with cocoa solids, cocoa butter and sugar.
> **Milk chocolate**: Made with cocoa solids, cocoa butter, sugar and milk.
> **White chocolate**: Made with cocoa butter, sugar and milk.

In the UK the percentage rating for dark chocolate must be 50 per cent or over.

Milk Chocolate

Milk chocolate must contain at least 25 per cent of cocoa. Its flavour is too mild to use as a baking ingredient in cakes, but it is a popular ingredient in buttercream for children's cakes. A mixture of plain and milk chocolate also makes a delicious 'semi-sweet' alternative in frostings and ganache. It can also be used as a drip, for a finishing decoration on a cake.

White Chocolate

White chocolate does not contain any cocoa solids, but is made from cocoa butter and has a percentage rating of at least 20 per cent. Some cheaper brands of white chocolate replace the cocoa butter content with vegetable oil. This can make the chocolate unstable, causing it to burn quickly when heated and resulting in it being difficult to set. Good quality white chocolate usually has a rating above 25 per cent. No vegetable oils have been added and it has a truer taste of chocolate. This can be used for frostings in the same way as milk chocolate.

White chocolate is a useful addition to buttercream, as it helps to stabilise the frosting in hotter weather. To make chocolate buttercream, add 300g (10½oz) of cooled, melted white chocolate to a batch of buttercream made

White chocolate is made from cocoa butter.

with 250g (9oz) of butter and 500g (17½oz) of icing sugar. The buttercream may be a little stiff once all the chocolate has been incorporated, so add a few drops of water to the mixture until the correct consistency is reached.

Ruby Chocolate

Ruby chocolate is relatively new to the market. It is sometimes referred to as the fourth type of chocolate. It was introduced in 2017 by a Belgian-Swiss company called Callebaut. It is believed to be manufactured from unfermented cocoa beans (or beans fermented for no more than three days), which then become red or purple after treating them with citric acid. The result is a creamy, 'fruity'-tasting chocolate. It has a richer, deeper flavour than white chocolate, but not as much as milk chocolate. It can be used in frostings as well as chocolate decorations.

Milk chocolate, due to the addition of milk, has a milder, creamier flavour.

Gold Chocolate

Gold chocolate has a delicate, toffee flavour. It has a higher cocoa percentage than white chocolate, and can be used both as a decoration as well as an ingredient in frostings, ganache or glazes.

Ruby chocolate is often known as the fourth type of chocolate.

Gold chocolate is a white chocolate blended with caramel.

Couverture Chocolate

Couverture chocolate is used by chocolatiers and professional bakers when making glazes, such as a pouring ganache or for decorations. It needs to be 'tempered' before using. This process is done to ensure the chocolate has a deep shine and a sharp 'snap' when broken. It also makes the chocolate easier to work with. Tempering is not necessary when using chocolate for making chocolate buttercream, ganache for fillings, or when making mirror glazes, but if a deep, glossy shine is required for decorative finishes, it is worth taking the time to temper the chocolate.

Couverture is a chocolate that contains a higher percentage of cocoa butter than baking or eating chocolate.

HOW TO TEMPER CHOCOLATE

Tempering is done by melting and cooling the chocolate and then warming it again to a specific temperature, according to the type of chocolate being used. There are various ways of tempering chocolate, but the following two methods can be easily done in a home kitchen. Neither method requires any specialist equipment. The first method uses a microwave and the second tempers the chocolate in a bain marie.

Tempering Chocolate in a Microwave
You will need:

Good quality chocolate that contains at least 32 per cent cocoa butter – dark, milk or white. Use callets or chopped chocolate

Microwave

Plastic microwavable bowl

Plastic or metal spoon or spatula

Palette knife

Thermometer

Hairdryer or heat gun

Method:

1. Begin by adding about two thirds of the chocolate to the plastic bowl. Heat in the microwave on half power for about 30 seconds.

2. Remove the bowl and stir well. Repeat this step until the chocolate has melted. Do not be tempted to increase the power, as chocolate can burn quickly.

3. When the chocolate has melted, check the temperature with the thermometer. It should be 40–45°C (105–115°F).

4. Gradually add small amounts of the remaining third of chocolate, whilst gently stirring. This will cool down the chocolate.

5. When the correct temperature has been reached the chocolate will be correctly tempered and ready to use. The temperature required differs for each chocolate type. For dark chocolate it needs to be 31–32°C (88–90°F), milk chocolate 29–30°C (84–86°F) and white chocolate 27–28°C (80–82°F).

6. Another way to check to see if the chocolate is tempered is to dip the end of a palette knife into the chocolate and leave it to one side for approximately five minutes. If the chocolate has started to set then it is tempered and ready to use. If it has not set, then it is still too warm to use.

7. If whilst working with the tempered chocolate it starts to cool and thicken, either a hairdryer or heat gun can be used to gently warm it. Check the temperature before continuing to use.

Tempering Chocolate in a Bain Marie
You will need:

Good quality chocolate that contains at least 32 per cent cocoa butter – dark, milk or white. Use callets or chopped chocolate

Stove top

Saucepan

Glass bowl (one that when placed into the saucepan does not touch the bottom)

Plastic or metal spoon or spatula

Palette knife

Thermometer

Hairdryer or heat gun

Method:

1. Heat a small amount of water in the saucepan up to a gentle simmer. Put two thirds of the chocolate into the glass bowl and then place the bowl on top of the saucepan. Gently stir until the chocolate has melted.

2. When the chocolate has melted, check the temperature with the thermometer. It should be 40–45°C (105–115°F).

3. Remove the glass bowl from the heat and wipe the underside to avoid water drops. Pour the melted chocolate into a plastic bowl.

4. Gradually add small amounts of the remaining third of chocolate, whilst gently stirring. This will cool down the chocolate. You may not need to add all the chocolate.

5. When the correct temperature has been reached the chocolate will be correctly tempered and ready to use. The temperature required differs for each chocolate type. For dark chocolate it needs to be 31–32°C (88–90°F), milk chocolate 29–30°C (84–86°F) and white chocolate 27–28°C (80–82°F).

6. Another way to check to see if the chocolate is tempered is to dip the end of a palette knife into the chocolate and leave to one side. If the chocolate has started to set after approximately five minutes, then it is tempered and ready to use. If it has not set, then it is still too warm to use.

7. If, whilst working with the tempered chocolate, it starts to cool and thicken, either a hairdryer or heat gun can be used to gently warm it. Check the temperature before continuing to use.

USING CHOCOLATE AS AN INGREDIENT FOR CAKE COVERINGS AND FILLINGS

Chocolate is a very versatile ingredient for cake coverings. It can be used as a quick and easy topping, simply by melting, cooling and pouring over a cake. When butter is added to the melted chocolate a softer coating is created that will not crack when the cake is cut into. Melted chocolate can also be added to any of the buttercreams described in Chapter 3. Adding chocolate also helps to stabilise buttercream in warmer weather – for example, when making a celebration or wedding cake that will be on display for a few hours.

In the colder months, a chocolate buttercream-coated cake can be stored in a cool room. It does not need to be refrigerated. During the festive season, this can be a huge bonus when space may be limited in the fridge.

PROJECT 7: CHOCOLATE YULE LOG

A chocolate yule log is a popular festive cake with all ages.

This is a popular cake to serve with all ages. It is easy to prepare so would be a good choice to make as a baking project with children. The buttercream is used as both the filling and coating for the chocolate Swiss roll in this project, but an alternative filling of whipped double cream, vanilla or white chocolate buttercream could be used instead. A simple dusting of icing sugar completes the finished log. The traditional decorations of holly leaves, berries and a robin are readily available from most supermarkets and cake-decorating suppliers during the festive season.

This buttercream recipe varies from the American buttercream recipe in Chapter 3 in that equal amounts of icing sugar and butter are used, rather than the 2:1 ratio. The American buttercream recipe could be used in this project as an alternative before adding the chocolate.

Equipment:
33 × 23cm (13 × 9in) Swiss roll tin
Baking parchment
Electric handheld or stand mixer

Ingredients:
For the cake:
4 large eggs
100g (3½oz) caster sugar
65g (2½oz) self-raising flour
40g (1½oz) cocoa powder

For the chocolate buttercream:
200g (7oz) dark chocolate, about 54 per cent cocoa solid
250g (9oz) butter, softened
250g icing sugar, plus extra to dust (powdered sugar)

Method:

1. Preheat the oven to 190°C/180°C fan/gas mark 5. Grease and line the Swiss roll tin with baking parchment.

2. Place eggs and caster sugar into a mixing bowl and whisk until very thick and creamy. The mixture is ready when it leaves a trail for about ten seconds after lifting out the whisk.

3. Sift in the flour and cocoa powder over the whisked eggs and carefully fold in with a spatula or metal spoon until evenly combined.

4. Turn the mixture into the prepared tin and gently tip it so that the mixture goes into the corners. Bake in the oven for twelve to fifteen minutes, or until springy to the touch.

5. Turn out the cake on to another sheet of baking parchment lightly sprinkled with caster sugar. Carefully remove the lining paper.

6. Make an incision about 1cm (0.4in) in from the long edge near you, being careful not to cut through the cake: this makes it easier to roll up.

7. Fold in the indented end and roll it up tightly, with the baking parchment inside the roll. Place on a wire rack and allow to cool completely.

8. Meanwhile, make the icing. Melt the chocolate in a bowl over a pan of hot water, stirring until fully melted. Remove from the pan and allow to cool.

9. Beat the butter and icing sugar together until pale and fluffy, then gradually beat in the cooled chocolate.

To complete the cake, carefully unroll the Swiss roll and spread with about one third of the buttercream. Carefully reroll without the paper. Cut off a wedge from one end, and place the cake on a plate or board with the cut-off piece butting up to one side.

Use the remaining chocolate buttercream to cover the cake. Either pipe the buttercream with a star nozzle attached, or use a small palette knife to create a bark effect along the lengths of the log. Use a small knife to spread the chocolate in a circular movement over the ends of the log.

Chill for about one hour before decorating with chocolate toadstools and other decorations, then lightly dust with icing sugar just before serving.

Chocolate Toadstool Decorations

Chocolate toadstool decorations.

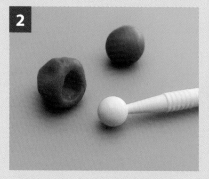

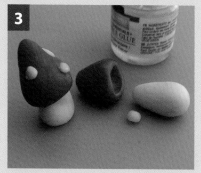

1 These decorative little toadstools can be made with sugarpaste, marzipan or, as shown here, in modelling chocolate. Take some white modelling chocolate and roll it into three smooth balls. Then form these into cone shapes for the stalks. Reserve a little of the white paste and colour the remaining paste red using either edible food paste or powder colour.

2 To make the toadstool caps, use the red paste and again start with smooth balls and then mould them into bell shapes. They can all be slightly different in shape. Use a ball tool to indent the base of each cap before placing it on to a stalk.

3 If the paste has dried a little, brush edible glue into the indent and then place each cap on to a stalk. Roll out the remainder of the white paste and use it to make the spots. This can be done either by rolling little balls of paste then flattening them with your finger, or by using a small cutter.

GANACHE

Another popular chocolate covering and cake filling is ganache. It has just two ingredients – chocolate and cream. Dark, milk and white chocolate can all be used to make ganache. Any chocolate brand can be used, but a good quality chocolate with a fat content of around 50 per cent will give a much better result. Chocolate with a higher percentage may be a little bitter for most tastes. Use cream with a high fat content, of at least 35 per cent. Whipping cream is ideal, but double cream is also a popular choice when making ganache. There are recipes that use single cream or even just water, but then the mixture is more prone to splitting and may have a dull, grainy appearance. Ganache should be smooth and shiny.

Ganache can be used when at pouring consistency as a coating or a drip for a cake. When cooled at room temperature the texture will resemble smooth peanut butter, and at this stage it can be used as both a cake filling and a covering. Ganache can also be whisked, which creates a light, fluffy mixture that can be used as both a filling and a topping. When refrigerated until firm, the mixture can be scooped and rolled to make truffles or other decorations.

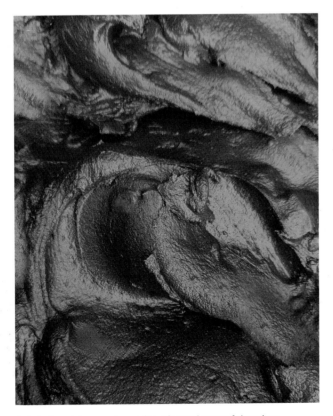

A dark chocolate ganache made with equal parts of chocolate and cream.

Ratios of Chocolate to Cream

The ratio refers to the amount of chocolate that is used with the quantity of cream. These quantities of chocolate and cream vary depending upon the type of chocolate being used. So as an example, a dark chocolate ganache for topping a 20cm (8in) round cake will need 150g (5½oz) dark chocolate and 150g cream. The ratio will be 1:1. When using milk chocolate, a ratio of 2:1 is required, which is 200g (7oz) milk chocolate and 100g (3½oz) of cream.

Here is a basic ratio guide for making ganache:

Dark chocolate 1:1

Milk chocolate 2:1

White chocolate 3:1

If a firmer ganache is required for a cake coating or making truffles then the ratios can be adjusted:

Dark chocolate 2:1

Milk chocolate 2.5:1

White chocolate 3.5:1

Two Methods for Making Ganache

Using the Hob

Chop the chocolate finely. The chocolate will melt more quickly and evenly. Place in a heat-proof bowl.

Heat the cream over a medium heat until it is simmering and tiny bubbles are beginning to appear around the edge of the pan – but it must not be boiling. Allow to cool if it overheats.

Pour the hot cream over the chocolate and leave it undisturbed for a minute.

Using a heat-proof spatula, begin to stir the ganache gently from the centre, slowly working outwards. Do not stir too quickly or vigorously. Keep stirring until all the chocolate is incorporated and the mixture is smooth and glossy.

Using the Microwave

Put the chopped chocolate and cream into a heat-proof bowl.

Heat on full power for ten to fifteen seconds, then stir gently with a heat-proof spatula.

Continue heating in ten-second bursts, and then continue stirring until the chocolate has almost melted. Remove from the microwave.

Continue stirring gently until the chocolate has fully melted and combined.

Using Ganache

When using ganache as a glaze, the chocolate should be tempered first in order to achieve a deep shine. Have the cake or cakes ready, frosted and chilled. Place on to a raised wire cake rack with a plate or tray underneath, and apply the ganache glaze whilst it is still of pouring consistency.

If using the ganache as a cake filling, leave it to cool for ten minutes. It will begin to thicken and become the consistency of peanut butter. At this stage it will be easier to apply and spread on to the cake.

Whipped ganache makes a delicious light cake coating and filling.

Use firm, refrigerated ganache to make truffles.

If whipped ganache is required, allow the mixture to cool to spreadable consistency. Use either an electric hand whisk or a stand mixer with a whisk attachment. Once whipped the ganache will be paler and will have a thick, creamy consistency.

If a firm ganache is needed for making decorations or truffles, place the ganache into an airtight container, such as an ice-cream tub. Lay clingfilm directly over the surface and allow to cool. Place the lid on the container and refrigerate for at least an hour before using.

Buttery Ganache

This type of ganache is simply – as the name suggests – a ganache with butter added. The result is a delicious, rich and fudgy-textured frosting that can be used either as a topping, filling or both.

The butter and chocolate are melted together either over a bain marie or in the microwave before adding the cream. Stir with a spatula until fully combined. Allow the mixture to cool until it reaches the consistency of peanut butter. For coating the top and sides of a 20cm (8in) cake, the quantities needed are 300g (10½oz) dark chocolate, 150g (5½oz) unsalted butter, and 150g of whipping or double cream.

Adding Flavours to Ganache

Flavours can be added to ganache in various ways. Use the hob method for making ganache. Bring the cream up to a gentle boil, add the infusion, then remove the pan from the heat, cover with a lid and allow to infuse for five minutes. Strain the cream before continuing to follow the ganache recipe.

Suggestions for infusions are lemon, lime and orange zest, split vanilla pods and their seeds, or culinary lavender.

Flavourings such as coffee granules, fruit powders or orange and coffee liqueurs can be added to the hot cream before pouring over the chocolate, but they do not need to infuse or be strained. When using liqueurs reduce the amount of cream used in the recipe by the amount of liqueur being used. For example, when making a dark chocolate ganache infused with an orange liqueur for topping and filling a 20cm (8in) cake you will need 300g (10½oz) dark chocolate, 260ml (8fl oz) whipping cream and 40ml (1½fl oz) orange liqueur.

A variety of flavours can be added to ganache.

Extracts such as vanilla, coffee and lemon, which are oil-based, can be added to the finished ganache. As they are very concentrated flavourings, only a very small quantity is required. The basic ganache recipe does not need to be adjusted.

Colouring Ganache

White chocolate ganache can be coloured easily using either an oil-based edible paste colour or edible dust colours. Add the colour when the ganache is still warm as it is easier to blend. Water-based colours must not be used as they will split the ganache.

Storing Ganache

A ganache-covered cake can be kept in a cake box at room temperature for two days. If the ganache needs to be stored for future use, then cover and seal in an air-tight container. It will keep in the fridge for two weeks, or can be frozen for three months. Ganache becomes very firm in the fridge. Unless it is going to be used for truffles, it will need to come back up to room temperature and soften before it can be used as a cake covering.

Trouble-Shooting Tips for Ganache

Ganache is an emulsion, just like mayonnaise, where oil and water are blended together. So although it is easy to make, it can be temperamental!

Ganache has separated: This usually happens when the cream is too hot whilst being added to the chocolate. As soon as the cream is steaming, remove from the heat. Stop stirring as soon as the emulsion has formed. To repair, add a little hot milk, and stir well until emulsified again.

Oil is on the surface of the ganache: This sometimes happens when double cream has been used instead of whipping cream, or when butter is added to the chocolate. To repair, try adding a little warm milk, as above.

The ganache is grainy: This sometimes happens when the ganache has been beaten too vigorously or for too long. To repair, try warming the ganache gently over a bain marie and use either a whisk or electric hand blender to disperse the fat.

The ganache is too soft: If the ganache is too soft when it has set, too much cream was used, or not enough chocolate added. Warm the ganache gently over a bain marie and add more cooled, melted chocolate.

Use edible colour dusts or oil-based paste colours for white ganache.

PROJECT 8: TRIPLE-CHOCOLATE DRIP CAKE

Triple-chocolate drip cake.

This rich and indulgent chocolate cake is a popular choice of celebration cake for all ages. The filling used is a whipped, dark chocolate ganache. Chocolate buttercream could be used as an alternative filling if preferred. Milk chocolate ganache is used to coat the top and sides. The drip is made with dark chocolate ganache. As the filling and coating are very rich, a simple chocolate sponge recipe with a firm texture has been used in this recipe. This will counteract the richness of the ganache as well as provide a firm sponge that is easier to decorate.

Once the cake has been filled, the remaining whipped ganache can be used to pipe swirls on the top of the finished cake. The milk and dark ganache from the coating and the drip can be refrigerated and used to make truffles for the final decoration.

Ingredients:
For the cake:
500g (17½oz) unsalted butter
500g (17½oz) light brown soft sugar
9–10 medium eggs (500g weight in the shell)
400g (14oz) self-raising flour
100g (3½oz) cocoa powder
1tsp vanilla extract

For the sugar syrup (optional):
100g (3½oz) caster sugar

For the filling:
300g (10½oz) dark chocolate (use 54 per cent cocoa solids)
300ml (10fl oz) whipping cream

For the topping and coating:
400g (14oz) milk chocolate (use 33 per cent cocoa solids)
200ml (7fl oz) whipping cream

For the chocolate drip:
80g (3oz) dark chocolate (use 54 per cent cocoa solids)
80ml (4fl oz) whipping cream

Making Sugar Syrup

To ensure the cake remains moist, a sugar syrup can be applied to the cake layers. To make this, place 100g (3½oz) caster sugar and 100ml (2½fl oz) water into a pan over a high heat, and stir until the sugar has dissolved and the syrup starts to boil. Pour into a bowl and allow to cool.

Equipment:
2 × 20cm (8in) round cake tins
Tall cake side scraper
Palette knife
Angled palette knife
Turntable
Piping bags – one large with a piping nozzle and one small for the drip
Piping nozzle

Method:
For the cake:
1. Preheat the oven to 170°C/150°C fan/gas mark 3, and line two 20cm (8in) cake tins with baking parchment.
2. In a stand mixer or a large bowl, beat together the unsalted butter and light brown soft sugar until light and fluffy.
3. Add the eggs, flour, cocoa powder and vanilla extract, and beat again until fully combined – but do not over-beat. Divide the mixture equally between the two tins.
4. Bake the cakes in the oven for 50–60 minutes, or until baked through. Leave the cakes to cool in the tins for ten minutes, then take out and leave to cool fully on a wire rack.
5. Using either a large serrated knife or a cake-cutting wire, level the tops if they are slightly domed. Then divide each cake into two, to give four layers.

For the filling:

Using either the hob or microwave method, make the chocolate ganache filling. Use either a stand mixer with a whisk attachment, or a large bowl with a hand whisk to whip the ganache until it is pale and fluffy. Cover the surface with clingfilm, making direct contact with the ganache, and set aside whilst preparing the cakes for filling.

Apply a small amount of whipped ganache to the centre of one of the cake boards to secure the cake to the board, and position the bottom half of the first cake on to the board. Brush with sugar syrup if you are using this. Using a large palette knife, spread the cake with some of the whipped ganache, then position the remaining half of the first cake upside down on top. Gently press down and check the level with a spirit level. Brush with sugar syrup.

Add the next layer of filling, then place the bottom half of the second cake on top and brush with sugar syrup. Any remaining syrup can be stored in the fridge for up to two weeks. Add the final layer of filling. Place the remaining cake layer on top but upside down to give a flat surface. Check that the cake is level. Place it in the fridge for 20 to 30 minutes to firm up. Cover with the remaining filling, then set it aside for decorating later.

For the milk chocolate ganache coating:

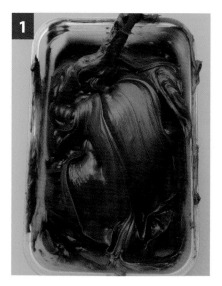

Prepare the milk chocolate ganache for the coating, using one of the methods given above. Allow to cool at room temperature until it reaches the consistency of peanut butter.

To ensure the sides of the cake are straight, use a serrated knife and trim away about ½cm (0.2in) from all sides of the cake. Clean up any crumbs that have dropped around the base of the cake.

Place the cake on a turntable if there is one available. Use a large palette knife to apply a thin layer of ganache to the sides and top to act as a crumb coat. Smooth out the ganache, making sure that none goes beyond the cake board. Place in the fridge for approximately ten minutes to allow the ganache to set.

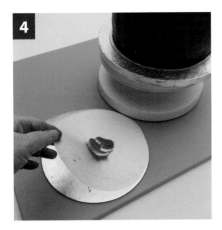

Apply a small amount of ganache to the silver side of the second cake board and place the parchment circle on top. Apply a very thin layer of ganache to the top of the cake. Place the cake board, parchment paper side down, on the top of the cake. Use the side scraper to check that the base board and top cake board are in line with each other.

Gently hold down the top cake board with one hand and apply a generous layer of ganache in an upward motion around the sides of the cake.

Hold the side scraper against the top and bottom cake boards and scrape away the excess ganache. Some gaps or dents usually appear, so repeat, adding more ganache, and scrape around the cake again until the sides are smooth.

Place the cake back into the fridge for approximately fifteen to twenty minutes until it is firm and can be touched without leaving finger marks. Remove from the fridge. Gently remove the top cake board using the tip of a sharp knife between the ganache and the cake board. Twist the knife gently to release the board and peel away the parchment paper.

If the top of the cake looks rough and uneven use an offset spatula to spread on some extra ganache. Fill in any holes and smooth the surface. Place in the fridge to set completely. Cover and refrigerate the remaining ganache to make truffle decorations later.

For the chocolate drip:

Make the dark chocolate ganache using one of the methods described above, or as an alternative for making a smaller quantity, melt the chocolate and cream together in the microwave. Remove and stir after every fifteen seconds until the chocolate has almost completely melted. Continue stirring until smooth.

Pour the ganache into a small piping bag. Remove the cake from the fridge and place back on the turntable. Cut off the tip of the piping bag.

Gently squeeze the ganache on to the edge of the cake and nudge it gently over the sides. Increasing the pressure on the bag will result in longer drips. Either give consistent pressure for even-length drips, or vary them. Return the cake to the fridge for 20 to 30 minutes to set fully.

For the final decoration:

Use the remaining milk or dark ganache to make into truffles.

Scoop out the mixture with a teaspoon and quickly roll into even-sized balls. These can be left plain, or dusted with either cocoa powder or gold edible dust. Refrigerate until required.

To create a neat border of sprinkles, wrap a strip of acetate around the cake, leaving the base uncovered. Press the sprinkles into the base using an angled palette knife. Place the cake back in the fridge for fifteen minutes, before removing the acetate.

Gently squeeze the piping bag of ganache on to the edge of the cake and nudge it gently over the sides.

If the ganache filling has been refrigerated, allow to come back to room temperature and re-whisk until light and fluffy. Place in a piping bag with a piping nozzle attached.

Pipe even swirls of ganache around the top of the cake.

Decorate with truffle balls, sprinkles, or other decorations.

Store at room temperature in a cake box. The cake will keep for at least three days and can be frozen for up to three months.

Use a piping bag with an open star nozzle to pipe swirls on the top of the cake.

MODELLING CHOCOLATE

Although modelling chocolate is mostly used for making small decorations and figures, it also makes a delicious cake covering. It can be used as a base coat under a top layer of sugarpaste, as an alternative to marzipan, or as a quick covering applied as a single layer. It only has two ingredients – chocolate and syrup. The syrup ingredient could be either golden, corn, maple, agave nectar or liquid glucose. Golden syrup or liquid glucose is the most popular choice due to cost and availability.

The amount of syrup needed varies according to the type of chocolate used. As an approximate guide when using either white, milk or ruby chocolate, the ratio is 2:1 – for example, 200g (7oz) of chocolate mixed with 100g (3½oz) syrup. When using dark chocolate with 55 per cent cocoa solids, the ratio is 1:1, which would be 100g chocolate with 100g of syrup.

How to Make Modelling Chocolate

Ingredients:

200g (7oz) chocolate
100g (3½oz) golden/corn syrup or glucose (200g (7oz) if using dark chocolate)

Method:

1. Slowly melt the chocolate in either a microwave or a bain marie. Take care not to overheat the chocolate above 35°C/95°F.
2. Warm the syrup until it is slightly runny and approximately the same temperature as the chocolate.
3. Add the syrup to the chocolate and stir in slowly using a spatula, until completely combined. The mixture will begin to stiffen and pull away from the sides of the bowl.
4. Roll out a large sheet of clingfilm, pour the paste on to the clingfilm, and spread out using the spatula.
5. Cover completely with the clingfilm and leave to cool at room temperature for at least twelve hours before using. Alternatively, allow to cool a little before transferring to the fridge for at least an hour.
6. Only break off the amount required, before kneading to make the paste malleable and smooth. If the paste is very hard and stiff it can be softened in the microwave for five seconds. If it is too warm and sticky then allow it to cool in the fridge.
7. Over-kneading the paste will naturally cause it to melt and become sticky, so try to avoid over-handling it.

Using Modelling Chocolate

The paste can be rolled out in the same way as sugarpaste. Use either icing sugar or cornflour to prevent it sticking. Using modelling chocolate as a cake covering is much easier on smaller cakes or as one layer on a larger cake top, as the paste has a tendency to crack and break easily if larger sheets are rolled out.

It is a very good paste to use for small models and flowers as it moulds easily, holds its shape, and sticks to itself without the addition of edible glue. Any joins and seams can also be smoothed out easily.

Colouring Modelling Chocolate

Use an oil-based colour paste, such as a brand called 'Colour Mill', or edible food dusts to colour the finished modelling

Modelling chocolate can be purchased ready-made.

Homemade modelling chocolate is quick and easy to prepare.

Colour modelling chocolate with either an oil-based colour paste or edible dusts.

paste. A range of bright colours can be made when using white chocolate modelling paste. Black is easier to achieve using dark chocolate modelling paste. Colour small quantities of modelling paste at a time as it must be kneaded in quickly to avoid overhandling and the paste becoming sticky and unworkable. If this happens, rewrap it in clingfilm and place it in the fridge for ten minutes. Examples of chocolate roses and other decorations made using modelling chocolate can be found in Chapter 9 'Finishing Touches'.

Chocolate Mirror Glaze

A simple shiny glaze can be made with a pourable chocolate ganache. To achieve a high shine on the cake covering, a good quality tempered couverture chocolate must be used.

An alternative recipe for a glaze with a high shine is to make a mirror glaze. This glaze is often seen on French patisserie cakes and desserts called 'entremets'. These are made using a variation of cake sponge layers, mousses, jellies and jams or curds. The mirror glaze is the final element that is poured over the top and sides to completely encase the filling.

The ingredients needed are cocoa powder, cream, sugar, water and gelatine. It is the addition of gelatine that gives the glaze its glossy mirror-like shine. Gelatine is available to buy in sheets known as leaf gelatine or as a powder. Both are readily available in most supermarkets. Powdered gelatine is more economical.

Some recipes for mirror glaze include melted chocolate and condensed milk. These tend to produce a thicker glaze, which is less likely to show imperfections, such as tiny bubbles, but they sometimes lose their high shine after a day or two, and a thicker jelly coating may not be as appealing to eat.

Mirror-glazed cakes can be refrigerated uncovered and will keep well for a few days.

PROJECT 9: MIRROR-GLAZED CHOCOLATE MOUSSE CAKES WITH SALTED CARAMEL

Mirror-glazed chocolate mousse cakes with salted caramel centres.

Although mirror-glazed cakes and entremets are usually seen in high-end patisserie shops and tea rooms, a simple glaze can be made in a home kitchen and used to coat a large cake or smaller individual cakes that have been frosted with either buttercream or ganache. Mirror glazing on an unfrosted cake does not work as the glaze sinks into the sponge. A firmer sponge, such as a Madeira or genoise, will be easier to handle when applying the buttercream or ganache. The surface needs to be as even and smooth as possible, as any imperfections will be highly visible on the finished cake. The cakes will need to be refrigerated or frozen before applying the glaze.

In this project, fatless sponges have been used and topped with a chocolate mousse, before being encased in a mirror glaze. They would be perfect as part of an afternoon tea or used as a dessert. Silicone moulds are easily available from online stores or specialist cook shops. They allow the frozen mousse to be easily unmoulded, and give a smooth finish to the top of the cakes.

The three components to this cake can all be made separately ahead of time, or the sponge and mousse can be made on the same day, assembled in the silicone mould and frozen. They will keep for up to three months in the freezer. Adding a little salted caramel to the filling is optional, but gives an element of surprise as well as another texture to the finished cake. An alternative filling could be an orange curd used with the chocolate mousse, and an orange-flavoured chocolate sponge base.

Chocolate Sponge Cake Base
Equipment:

Swiss roll tin
Baking parchment
Whisk (hand or electric)
Silicone moulds, 6cm (2.3in)
Pastry cutter, 58mm
Wire cooling rack
Sieve
Palette knife

Ingredients:

60g (2oz) self-raising flour
3tbsp cocoa powder
3 eggs
75g (2½oz) golden caster sugar

Method:

1. Heat the oven to 220°C/200°C fan/gas mark 7. Line a Swiss roll tin with parchment paper.
2. Sift the flour and cocoa powder together over a large piece of parchment paper (slightly larger than the tin) and set aside.
3. Add the eggs and sugar into a bowl or the bowl of a stand mixer. Using either an electric whisk or the whisk attachment, beat the eggs and sugar together for five minutes until pale and very thick.

4. Tip in the flour and cocoa-powder mix. Keep the paper for later. Gently fold the flour into the mixture, using either a spoon or spatula, until completely incorporated and no flour lumps are visible.
5. Pour the mixture into the tin and gently spread out to the corners using a palette knife. Bake for nine to ten minutes until risen, and the cake springs back when gently pressed.
6. Tip out the sponge on to the saved piece of parchment paper, and gently peel away the lining paper, without tearing it. Replace the paper on the top of the sponge and allow to cool a little.
7. Whilst the sponge is still slightly warm, cut out six discs using the cutters. Cover and set aside for later.

Chocolate Mousse
Ingredients:

300g (10½oz) dark chocolate (50 per cent cocoa solids), callets or roughly chopped
450ml (17fl oz) whipping cream

Method:

1. Melt the chocolate either in a bain marie, on the hob or in the microwave, then set aside to cool a little.
2. Whip the cream until soft peaks form when the whisk is removed. Gently fold the melted chocolate into the whipped cream until combined. Transfer to a piping bag.

Filling (optional):

6tsp salted caramel paste (if using)

Mirror Glaze
Ingredients:

12g (½oz) powdered gelatine
100ml (3fl oz) whipping cream
225g (8oz) caster sugar
50g (2oz) cocoa powder

Method:

Pour 70ml of water into a small bowl. Sprinkle the powdered gelatine over the surface and set aside.

Pour 75ml of water into a saucepan, add the cocoa powder and whisk until the mixture becomes a smooth paste.

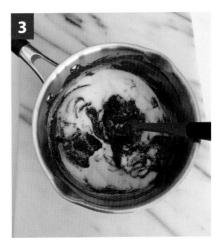

Gradually add the cream to the cocoa paste to loosen it up and smooth out any lumps. Stir in the sugar. Avoid vigorously stirring and whisking as this will produce bubbles.

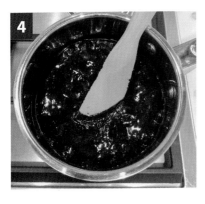

Place the pan on the heat and bring to the boil. As soon as the mixture comes to the boil, remove from the heat and stir in the gelatine. Continue stirring very gently until the gelatine has completely dissolved and the glaze is smooth and shiny.

Pour the glaze through a sieve into a jug. Cover with clingfilm, making sure it is in contact with the surface. Set aside to cool at room temperature. At this point the glaze can be kept in the freezer for up to three months.

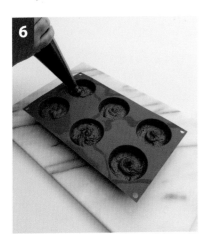

Ensure the silicone moulds are clean and dry. Pipe the chocolate mousse into each mould about three-quarters full. Tap the moulds gently on the work surface to remove any air pockets. If using salted caramel paste, spoon one teaspoon into the centre of each mould.

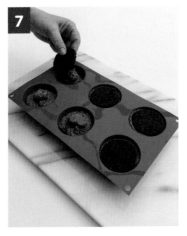

Place a disc of cake sponge on to the top of each mould and press gently to ensure the surface is flat and level. Place in the freezer for four hours, or leave overnight (they can also be stored in the freezer at this point for up to three months).

Assembly:

When ready to glaze, have a wire cooling rack ready over a baking tray with sides. Place two angled palette knives into a jug of hot water and have the presentation plate nearby.

Remove the mousses from the moulds and space them out on the wire rack. Place both palette knives under the first mousse to be coated. Pour the glaze over one mousse at a time. Start in the middle and spiral outwards in one movement for complete coverage.

As soon as the glaze has been applied to each mousse, remove each one from the wire rack with the warm, undried palette knives, and place them on the presentation plate. Dip the knife back into the hot water between moving each mousse.

Whilst the mousse is still wet, apply some gold leaf to the top of each mould. Keep in the fridge for up to two days, uncovered.

CHAPTER 6

FRUITS AND NUTS

· · · · · · · · · · · · · · · · ·

One of the quickest and easiest ways to cover a cake is to use fruits and nuts. In the summer months, a cake using fresh summer berries piled high on a fresh cream-covered sponge is both quick to assemble and always a crowd pleaser. During the cooler months when fresh fruits are no longer in season, dried or candied fruits are equally decorative and can transform a plain-looking cake into an edible work of art. Nuts are readily available all year round. Varieties such as walnuts, pecans, almonds, macadamia nuts, brazil nuts and pistachios can provide both pattern and texture to cake toppings.

FRESH FRUITS

The key to success when using fresh fruit for cake decorating is to use very fresh, blemish-free fruits. Some fruits such as strawberries, raspberries and blueberries have a short shelf and can be easily damaged, so select fruit that is not over-ripe. If the fruits are going to be stored in the fridge for a few days, do not wash them and keep any leaves intact. Preserving soft fruits using a vinegar or citric acid bath may have a detrimental effect on the fruits as they absorb moisture, making them very soft and unusable. It is better to clean and prepare the fruits just before using.

Soft fruits, such as strawberries and raspberries, tend to lose their shape and become very soft when frozen, which would make them unsuitable as a cake topping. However, the fruits can be puréed and made into a coulis, or used as part of the cake filling by folding into fresh cream or buttercream. Berries with a skin, such as redcurrants, blueberries and blackcurrants, keep their shape a little better and can be used as part of a fruit medley cake topper.

Always choose fresh, blemish-free berries.

PROJECT 10: SUMMER BERRIES CELEBRATION CAKE

A perfect cake for a summer party.

This would be a perfect cake for a summer party. It is generously filled with whipped Chantilly cream and chopped fresh summer berries. The top is piled high with more fresh berries, meringue kisses and white chocolate-coated strawberries. Additional decorations such as mint leaves, gold leaf or small edible flowers could also be used. As fresh cream is used in this cake it must be assembled on the day of the party.

If the cake needs to be prepared a day or two before, then an alternative filling and coating of white chocolate ganache could be used (see page 7). The sponges can be made in advance and kept in the freezer for up to three months. If using meringue kisses, these can also be made ahead of time and will keep in an air-tight container for up to two weeks.

Instructions on how to make the meringue kisses can be found in Chapter 9 'Finishing Touches'.

Ingredients:
For the cake:
300g (10½oz) butter, at room temperature
300g (10½oz) caster sugar
300g (10½oz) self-raising flour
6 medium eggs, lightly beaten
1tbsp vanilla bean paste

For the Chantilly cream:
900ml (33fl oz) double cream
1 heaped tbsp icing sugar
2tsp vanilla bean paste

For the filling and topping:
300g (10½oz) good quality berry jam, either strawberry or raspberry (at room temperature)
1kg (2lb) summer berries – strawberries, raspberries, blueberries, blackberries
Apricot glaze (1tbsp sieved apricot jam, 1tsp water, heated to melt the jam)

Optional extras:
Meringue kisses
Chocolate-coated strawberries
Edible flowers

Equipment:
2 × 23cm (9in) tins, greased and lined with baking parchment
Large cake board, plate or cake stand for serving
Cake-cutting wire or serrated bread knife

Method:
1. Heat oven to 180°C/160°C fan/gas mark 4.
2. Beat the butter, sugar and vanilla in either a stand mixer with a paddle attachment, or by hand until the mixture is very light, pale and fluffy.
3. Whisk the eggs lightly in a separate jug before gradually adding to the mixture. Use a spatula to scrape down the sides of the bowl after each addition, until incorporated.
4. Fold in the flour by hand using either a silicone spatula or large metal spoon. Then divide the mixture between the tins and bake in the oven for 30 minutes or until the cakes come away from the sides and a skewer or tooth pick inserted into the centre comes out clean.
5. Remove and allow to cool in the tin for five minutes before turning out on to a wire rack. Peel away the parchment paper and leave the cakes to cool completely before assembling.
6. Prepare the fruit. Gently and quickly rinse the berries. Discard any damaged fruits and leave to drain on kitchen paper. Set aside about five large strawberries and equal amounts of other berries to use on the top of the cake. Slice the remaining strawberries, halve the larger raspberries and blackberries, but leave the blueberries intact.
7. Prepare the sponges for filling. Trim the tops of each cake if they have domed, using either a bread knife or cake-cutting wire. Then, using the same knife or cake wire, split each sponge horizontally to make four sponge layers.
8. Make the Chantilly cream. Whip the double cream with the icing sugar and vanilla until it holds its shape. Decant the cream into a large piping bag, fitted with an open-star piping nozzle.
9. Smooth a little cream on the centre of the cake board or stand. Place the bottom cake layer on top. Use a spatula to spread a thin layer of jam on the sponge, then spread or pipe on a generous layer of cream.
10. Arrange a third of the mixed fruit into the middle and gently spread this out evenly, avoiding the edges. Repeat with two more of the cake layers and mixed fruit.
11. For the top layer, add the sponge and jam, then neatly pipe the cream over. Add the reserved whole fruits and other decorations if using. Brush the fruits with some apricot glaze. Refrigerate until ready to serve. Eat within a few hours.

DRIED FRUITS

Using dried fruits in cake making, both as an ingredient and decoration, has long been a popular choice for the home baker. Readily available in most supermarkets, they are an affordable store cupboard favourite, particularly when fresh fruits are out of season.

Traditional dried fruits such as raisins, currants, sultanas and apricots, have been part of the staple diet across the Mediterranean and Middle East for thousands of years. Fruits were left to dry out in the hot sun before being stored for consumption throughout the year. Today, as well as air drying, large heated wind tunnels called dehydrators are used to dry fruit on an industrial scale before they are exported across the world. Turkey is one of the world's largest exporters of dried fruit.

In addition to the drying process, many fruits, such as cranberries and blueberries, are sweetened with sugar syrup before drying. This enhances their flavour as well as acting as a preservative. Some dried fruits, such as apricots and golden raisins, are treated with sulphur dioxide, which retains the bright colour of the fruits, avoiding oxidisation. Although harmless to most, fruit processed in this way is best avoided by anyone suffering from asthma as it has been found to induce attacks. Apricots are now available to buy as 'unsulphured'.

As well as dehydrating whole fruits, larger fruits such as mangoes and apples are sliced before drying. Fruits such as dates are also available to buy chopped after being dried. Another dried fruit product is 'fruit leather'. This is made by pouring the puréed fruit on to a drying rack and drying in a commercial dehydrator.

A popular ingredient to use in baking is freeze-dried fruit. This process is where fresh fruit is frozen and placed in a drying chamber under a vacuum. The chamber is then heated, and all the moisture in the fruit is evaporated. This process gives the fruit a very light, crispy texture with an intense flavour. The freeze-dried fruit can also be easily made into fruit powders, by grinding in a food processor. The advantage of using freeze-dried fruit as an addition to a cake filling or topping is that it does not add any additional moisture and can be easily folded into buttercream or chocolate without affecting its consistency. Whole freeze-dried fruits can be placed directly on a cake topping, or crumbled on to the top to add an additional flavoursome decoration.

Raisins, currants, sultanas and apricots.

Apricots are now available to buy as 'unsulphured'.

How to Dehydrate Apple or Pear Slices in a Food Dehydrator

Domestic dehydrators and air fryers with a dehydrating function are becoming increasingly popular in the home kitchen. This is an easy way to preserve apples and pears. As well as being a delicious snack, they can also be used as a decorative cake topper. It will take about eight hours to dehydrate the apples in the food dehydrator.

You will need:

Food dehydrator or air fryer with a dehydrate function
Apples or pears
Mandolin or a very sharp knife
Acidulated water (bowl of water with either ½tsp vinegar or 1tbsp lemon juice added)
Glass jars for storage

Method:

1. Slice the apples or pears approximately ½cm (0.2in) thick; there is no need to peel or core. Place the slices into the acidulated water straightaway to minimise the chances of the slices browning.
2. Leave in the water for five minutes, then remove and lay out on to a clean tea towel and pat dry.
3. Place the slices on the dehydrator racks. Take care not to overlap the slices.
4. Place the racks into the dehydrator. Set the temperature to 55°C/131°F and set the timer for seven hours. After this time the slices should be dry and feel leathery. Continue drying for another hour if crisper slices are required.
5. When the slices are dry, remove the racks and allow to cool at room temperature for ten minutes. Once the slices are completely cold, transfer to glass jars and seal tightly.
6. Store away from direct light or heat. The slices will keep well for at least six months.

Dried apple slices.

FROSTED FRUIT

Another quick and easy way to prepare fruits for decorating is to frost them. This gives a crystal, snow-tipped look to fruits, so it is a perfect way to embellish Christmas or winter-themed cakes. Berries and fruits with a skin, such as grapes, work well as their juices will not seep through the sugar and spoil the frosted effect. Dip each fruit into egg white, shake off the excess, then dip into caster sugar. Leave to dry on either an acetate or silicone sheet before using.

Frosted fruit.

CANDIED GLACÉ FRUIT

Glacé fruit, also known as crystallised or candied fruit, has been a method of preserving fruits for centuries. Although recipes for candied fruits vary around the world, the basic principle of steeping whole fruits, pieces or peel into a hot sugar syrup remains the same. The process absorbs the moisture from within the fruit and eventually preserves it. Candied fruits have a long shelf life of up to two years, making them a store-cupboard favourite.

Glacé cherries and candied peel are the most popular candied fruits to use in the UK, both for cake decorating and as an ingredient in fruit cakes. Glacé cherries are available to buy in a variety of colours, usually due to food colouring being added, but naturally coloured glacé fruits are readily available too. Morello cherries, for example, are a deep burgundy colour and these are often used to decorate chocolate-based cakes.

Throughout the Middle East in countries such as Tunisia, Egypt and Lebanon, glacé fruits are eaten as sweet treats throughout the year. Many varieties of fruits are used, such as lemons, apricots, mandarins and figs. In France and Italy these fruits are highly prized as a dessert decoration, due to their bright colours and deep shine. They are particularly popular during festive seasons and celebratory events.

Making glacé fruits at home is a relatively simple task, but it can also be very time consuming, particularly when preparing larger fruits. Smaller fruits and peel can easily be prepared at home. Large glacé fruits are quite expensive, but when used as an embellishment very few fruits are required. Good quality candied fruits are available to buy online and recommendations for suppliers are given at the end of the book.

Candied fruit.

PROJECT 11: SICILIAN CASSATA CAKE

Sicilian cassata cake.

There are numerous recipes for this traditional Sicilian cake. It was originally eaten at Easter time to celebrate the end of Lent, but is now enjoyed on most festive occasions. It is composed of a round sponge cake moistened with fruit juices or liqueur, with marzipan sides and layered with ricotta cheese. The top is coated with icing before being decorated with a variety of candied fruits. Some recipes have chopped candied fruits or chocolate chips folded into the ricotta filling.

Ingredients:
For the sponge:
Butter, for greasing
150g (5½oz) plain flour, sifted, plus extra for dusting
6 eggs, at room temperature
150g (5½oz) caster sugar
Zest of 1 lemon

For the filling:
3tbsp limoncello or Grand Marnier
500g (17½oz) ricotta
150g (5½oz) caster sugar

For the marzipan:
500g ready-made marzipan
Green food colouring

For the icing:
200g (7oz) icing sugar
Juice of 1 lemon

For the decoration:
Selection of candied fruits

Equipment:
23cm (9in) springform cake tin
23cm (9in) cassata tin, or a sloping-sided 23cm (9in) pie tin lined with clingfilm

Method:
1. Heat the oven to 180°C/160°C fan/gas mark 4.
2. Butter and flour a 23cm (9in) springform cake tin.
3. Break the eggs into a bowl, beat for ten minutes, then add the caster sugar and zest, and beat until the mix forms a ribbon when poured.
4. Fold in the flour a third at a time, then pour into the tin and bake for 25–30 minutes.

To assemble and decorate the cassata:

For the marzipan sides, add a few drops of food colouring and knead until smooth and the colour has fully blended into the paste.

Roll out to 1cm (0.4in) thick on a surface dusted with icing sugar. Cut into 5cm (2in)-wide strips. Line a 23cm (9in) cassata tin, or a sloping-sided 23cm pie tin lined with clingfilm, then wrap the marzipan strips along the inside edge of the tin, slightly overlapping the ends and moulding it in to form a smooth layer.

Cut the cooled sponge across into three even slices. Put one slice in the base of the tin. It may need to be trimmed to fit. Then drizzle over a tablespoon of the limoncello. Mix the ricotta and sugar, then spread half of the mixture over the sponge. Repeat with another cake slice, limoncello and the remaining ricotta mixture. Top with the final cake slice and drizzle over the third tablespoon of limoncello. Turn out on to a serving plate and carefully lift off the tin and clingfilm.

For the icing, sift the icing sugar into a bowl, add half the lemon juice, and stir until smooth; then add the remaining sugar and juice. Ice the top of the cake, using a spatula to smooth out the surface, but leaving the marzipan sides uniced.

Decorate with the whole and cut candied fruits. Use royal icing to pipe a side design. Refrigerate for at least two hours before serving.

Crystallised Citrus Peel

Any citrus fruit can be used. Crystallised lemon slices and peel make a delicate decoration for a Madeira or sponge cake, and crystallised orange slices or peel are a popular topping for a carrot or passion cake.

Ingredients:
1 unwaxed lemon, lime, orange or grapefruit
50g (2oz) caster sugar
1 tbsp granulated sugar

Method:
1. Use a vegetable peeler to peel long strips of zest from the fruit and then use a sharp knife to slice it into very thin strips. Line a baking tray with baking parchment.
2. Place the sugar, 4tbsp of water and the juice of half the fruit into a small saucepan and heat gently, stirring until the sugar has dissolved. Once clear, add the zest and simmer for ten minutes or until the zest is translucent. Remove the peel from the syrup and leave to dry out on the prepared tray.
3. Toss the cool candied peel in the granulated sugar, before using as a decoration.

Crystallised fruits are prepared by being candied first and then dipped into sugar.

NUTS

Nuts are an extremely useful store-cupboard ingredient. Not only do they add texture and flavour to cake fillings, but they can be used as a quick decorative cake covering. They can be used whole and then glazed, or crushed to give a crunchy texture to cake tops and as a side covering. The most popular nuts to use for cakes are almonds, brazil nuts, coconuts, macadamia nuts, hazelnuts, pecans, pistachios and walnuts. They are readily available to buy either as whole nuts, chopped or ground. Although most are available to buy ready peeled, it is quite an easy task to dry roast or grill them to remove any papery skins. They can then be placed whole on top of a cake, using apricot jam to act as both the adhesive and the finishing glaze, as shown in Project 12, later in this chapter.

Almonds

Almonds are the most popular nuts to use in cake decorating. There are two varieties of almond: the bitter almond and the sweet almond. Bitter almonds are used to make almond oil and sweet almonds are used in baking. They are available to buy as whole nuts, skinned or unskinned. They are sometimes sold as 'flaked'. This means the almonds have been blanched to remove the skins and then finely sliced. 'Nibbed' almonds have also been blanched, but have been sliced across the length of the nut and then into sticks. Ground sweet almonds are a popular baking ingredient and can also be used to substitute flour when baking gluten-free cakes.

Almonds – whole, flaked, toasted and ground.

Brazil Nuts

Brazil nuts are the edible seeds of a large tree that is native to the Amazon. They can be eaten raw, or blanched. Although the shells are quite difficult to crack open, the nut inside is quite soft and creamy with a mild flavour. Brazils pair particularly well with dark chocolate. Dark-chocolate brazil nuts are a popular confection to buy ready-made. They provide a quick and attractive cake decoration for a rich chocolate cake.

Coconut

Coconuts have been used as a cake ingredient and decoration in the UK for many years. They are available to buy fresh as a whole nut or ready prepared in chunks. The flesh of the coconut is also sold dried in flakes, both natural and toasted as well as desiccated. Dessicated coconut is the dried and finely grated flesh of the coconut. Being naturally sweet, it is used as a flavouring as well as a decoration. Coconut cream and milk have gained in popularity in recent times as an ingredient in both savoury and sweet recipes.

Brazil nuts, macadamias, hazelnuts, pecans and walnuts are popular nuts to use in baking.

Dried coconut flakes and desiccated coconut.

Macadamia Nuts

Macadamia are tree nuts native to Australia. They have a similar taste to hazelnuts, but have a much smoother, creamy, almost buttery taste. Macadamias pair particularly well with white chocolate and coconut.

Hazelnuts

Hazelnuts are small tree nuts grown across Europe and America. They have a hard brown shell, but are usually sold as whole shelled nuts or chopped. The thin dark skin surrounding the nut is best removed before using, as it has a slightly bitter flavour. Although they can be eaten raw, the creamy flavour of the nut is enhanced by roasting. Hazelnuts have a natural affinity with dark chocolate, and confections such as the Italian recipes Gianduja and Nutella are extremely popular.

Pecan Nuts

Pecans are edible tree nuts native to America. They are related to walnuts, but due to their very high fat content, have a sweeter, creamier taste. Although similar in appearance to walnuts, pecans have a more uniform,

elongated shape that lends itself well to forming repeating patterns on top of cakes and pies. Pecans have become synonymous with the famous American dessert pecan pie, which has grown in popularity in the UK. Pecans have become extremely popular as a cake decoration and pair particularly well with caramel, maple syrup and toffee flavours.

Pistachios

Pistachios are grown and eaten across the Middle East as well as some parts of the Mediterranean. Although they are referred to as nuts, they are actually seeds called kernels. They are available to buy in their shells or unshelled, salted or natural. Nibbed pistachios are available in most stores selling Middle Eastern ingredients. They range in colour from a pale yellow to a vibrant, vivid green. They pair well with cream cheese and citrus frostings, particularly lime.

Pistachio kernels are available unshelled, shelled and nibbed.

Walnuts

Walnuts are one of the most popular nuts to eat in the UK. They can be eaten raw or used in baking. When used as a decoration or ingredient in a frosting or cake batter, they benefit from being lightly toasted to bring out their characteristic creamy, nutty flavour. This is easily done by heating in a dry frying pan for a few minutes until they begin to smell toasted. Walnuts do not keep as long as other nuts and should always be used within their 'use by' date. Older walnuts emit a rancid smell and have a bitter aftertaste.

Walnuts are the traditional ingredient and decoration for a coffee and walnut cake and pair particularly well with other mocha-flavoured cakes and desserts. They are also popular as a quick decoration for tea loaves and fruit cakes, containing bananas and dates.

PROJECT 12: FRUIT CAKE WITH A GLAZED NUT TOPPING

This is a quick and easy way to decorate a fruit cake. It is a perfect alternative for those who do not like the very sweet covering of marzipan and icing. This style of decoration will not have the same keeping qualities as a traditionally iced cake, but will store for up to twelve weeks. This recipe is enough to cover either an 18cm (7in) square or a 20cm (8in) round fruit cake.

Ingredients:

Selection of mixed nuts such as:

12 walnut halves

12 pecan nut halves

12 whole brazil nuts

12 whole blanched almonds

2tbsp sieved apricot jam

2tbsp brandy (optional)

Begin by preparing the nuts. Select undamaged whole or halved nuts. Spread out on a large dry frying pan and heat gently. They will begin to smell 'toasted' and will take on a light colour. Watch carefully, as they can quickly over-brown and burn. This may need to be done in batches. Allow the nuts to cool on a dry tea towel.

Prepare the glaze by warming the sieved apricot jam with the brandy (if using this) or water in a small saucepan. Stir until the jam has completely blended and the glaze is smooth and runny. Use a pastry brush to lightly coat the surface of the cake completely with the glaze.

3

4

Take a piece of parchment or baking paper the same size as the top of the cake, and arrange the nuts on the paper into the design of your choosing. It helps to have a 'practice run' of your design before placing the nuts on the sticky glaze. More or fewer nuts may be needed than anticipated.

Arrange the nuts on the surface of the cake and leave to set. Re-warm the remaining glaze and brush it over the nuts. Leave to set again.

5

Finish by securing a broad ribbon round the cake.

Candied Nuts

Some nuts are particularly well suited to being candied, such as whole pecans, walnuts and macadamia nuts. They can be enjoyed as a snack, and also look particularly attractive when used as a cake decoration. Less popular in the UK, but enjoyed in other parts of Europe, are candied chestnuts, known as 'marrons glacés'. The chestnuts are shelled and peeled before being cooked in a sugar syrup. They are a popular festive treat as well as being used to decorate desserts such as Mont Blanc.

Praline

A delicious confection that can be used either as a cake filling, by folding through buttercream, or as a cake topping or side decoration. Praline is made by adding nuts to a caramel before spreading out onto a baking tray lined with baking parchment or silicone mat. Any nuts, such as hazelnuts, almonds or pecans can be used, or a combination of nuts.

You will need:
100g (3½oz) granulated sugar
75g (2½oz) shelled hazelnuts (or alternative nuts)

1. Add the sugar and 4 tablespoons of water into a saucepan and place over a low heat.
   Slowly stir until the sugar dissolves and the syrup becomes clear.

2. Remove the spoon. Increase the heat and boil, without stirring, until the syrup is pale golden. (**Caution**: boiling sugar is extremely hot. Handle very carefully).

3. Add the nuts and swirl them gently around in the pan to coat them in the syrup. Avoid over-browning the syrup as the nuts may burn and the caramel will taste bitter. Quickly tip the mixture onto the baking sheet or silicone mat. Leave to cool and harden.

4. Once the praline has completely cooled, roughly chop with a sharp knife to create shards, or place into a strong plastic bag and crush with a rolling pin for smaller pieces. It can also be made into a praline crumb by giving it a quick blitz in a food processor.

5. Praline will keep for two to three days. To avoid it becoming sticky, it must be kept completely dry in an airtight container.

CHAPTER 7

ROYAL ICING

· · · · · · · · · · ·

Royal icing has long been regarded as the ultimate cake covering. It was originally known as 'egg-white icing' or 'snow icing'. In the mid to late nineteenth century it became very popular both as a cake covering and as a medium for piping and adding intricate decorations to cakes. When Queen Victoria married Prince Albert in 1840, their wedding cake was decorated using a white icing, so subsequently the icing was renamed in their honour and is now known as 'royal icing'.

The icing is made with a mixture of powdered icing sugar and egg whites. It produces a pure white smooth coating with a matte finish. It is also an extremely versatile icing as the consistency can be adjusted by either adding water to produce a runnier consistency for 'flooding' when making 'run-outs', or it can be stiffened by adding more powdered sugar so that the icing can be piped to create borders and patterns on to the cake. It is also extremely effective as a 'glue' for attaching pre-made sugar decorations to a cake.

Earlier recipes for the icing produced an extremely hard, brittle coating that was difficult to cut through and eat. Coupled with the introduction of sugarpaste as a cake covering, royal icing saw a decline in its popularity. However, in recent years it has seen a revival, particularly in the wedding-cake industry. Royal icing today, when used as a cake coating, usually contains glycerine. This is a 'humectant' substance, which when used as a food additive has the effect of retaining moisture and counteracting the hardness of the icing. The result is a sweet, 'melt-in-the-mouth' icing.

There are other advantages of having a royal iced cake. It is not affected by temperature, unlike buttercream that can quickly melt in the height of summer. Also with correct handling and suitable containers, royal-iced cakes are much easier to transport to venues due to their sturdiness.

Royal icing is easy to colour. Liquid colours or edible dusts are best to use if a dark colour is required, as adding larger quantities of gel or paste colours will prevent the icing from drying out completely. When pale colours are required and only a tiny dot of colour is used, then gel or paste colours will be fine to use.

READY-MIX ROYAL ICING

When using royal icing to 'flat ice' a cake, as in Projects 14 and 15 later in this chapter, or when using for piping lettering or intricate details, the consistency and strength of the icing is of paramount importance. Although homemade royal icing is easy to make, it does require a degree of accuracy. Even when following a reliable recipe, factors such as the freshness of the eggs, temperature and moisture in the atmosphere, as well as the brand of icing sugar, can all affect the finished result.

Royal icing powdered mixes are available to buy in most supermarkets. They have a long shelf life, making them convenient to store as well as avoiding any concerns about using raw fresh eggs. They produce consistently good results as all the ingredients have been pre-weighed and fully combined. Ready-mix royal icing also allows the convenience of being able to mix a very small quantity, such as when needed to pipe a small detail on top of a cake.

When stiffer icing is required for piping decorations with sharp details or when piping flowers using a flower nail, a 'firm peak' icing is required. This is achieved by simply adding extra icing sugar to the prepared royal icing.

'Soft peak' is where the icing will hold its shape, but when lifted with a palette knife or spatula the peaks on the icing bend over. At this stage the icing can be used to cover a cake using a 'free form' method, as in Project 13.

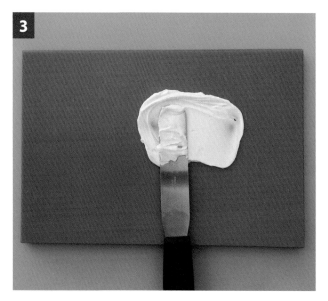

The smooth, or rubbed-down technique is used to eliminate any bubbles in the icing to create a smooth texture. The icing is 'smoothed out' on to a non-stick surface and 'paddled' using a large flat palette knife. This method is used when the icing must be as smooth and bubble free as possible, such as when 'flat icing' a cake, as in Projects 14 and 15.

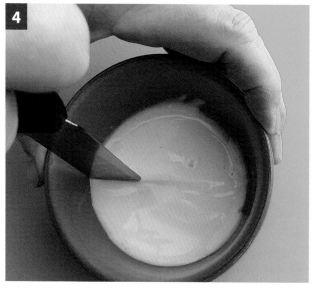

The consistency of icing known as 'run out', or 'flood out', is used to fill shapes that have had the outline piped, such as when piping lettering or numbers, as in Project 14. Cold water is added to the prepared royal icing until it reaches the consistency of single cream. A test for consistency is to draw a palette knife through the icing, and it should flow back together on a count of ten – so approximately ten seconds.

Homemade Royal Icing

This simple royal-icing recipe is ideal to use for a textured, free-form topping on Christmas and birthday cakes (as seen in Project 13). If using to cover a cake, it is important to remember to add some glycerine: this will avoid a very hard, brittle coating. If using for piping or when making 'run-outs' or panels as in Projects 14 and 15 later in this chapter, then glycerine must not be added to the icing.

Raw egg white can be substituted with powdered egg white. 5g (¼oz) of dried albumen is equivalent to one raw egg white. Most dried albumen powders have a shelf life of approximately six months and are available to buy in convenient 5g sachets.

The following recipe will be enough to make a textured covering for a 20cm (8in) round cake.

Ingredients:
600g (21oz) icing sugar (sieved)
3 medium egg whites or 15g (½oz) dried albumen (egg-white powder)
1tsp glycerine
1tbsp lemon juice (optional)

Method:
1. Begin by preparing the egg whites either by separating the whites from the yolks if using fresh eggs, or by reconstituting the dried albumen if using powdered egg whites.
2. To make the icing, lightly whisk the egg whites adding the sugar at intervals. Beat well until the icing forms soft peaks when the whisk is removed. Add the glycerine and the lemon juice, if using.

Royal Icing Consistencies

As previously mentioned, royal icing is very versatile. The consistency of the icing can be adjusted according to the usage. The starting point is to make a batch of icing following the recipe or packet instructions. At this stage it is known as 'soft peak', 'off peak', or normal.

PROJECT 13: SWIRLY TEXTURED CHRISTMAS CAKE

The cake will need to be covered with marzipan before the icing is applied. Follow the instructions in Project 4, Chapter 4. Frosted fruits, herbs and spices have been used for the top decoration. Instructions on how to make your own frosted decorations can be found in Chapter 6.

You will need:
20cm (8in) round fruit cake or 18cm (7in) square cake pre-covered with marzipan
600g (21oz) royal icing
Cake stand or board
Large palette knife
Side scraper (optional)
Selection of frosted fruits and herbs such as cranberries, rosemary and bay leaves, as well as dried orange slices, cinnamon sticks, star anise and cake decorator's pine cones

Method:
1. Add a small dot of royal icing to the centre of the cake board, before placing the marzipan-covered cake on top. This will secure it to the board and stop it moving around whilst icing the cake.
2. Prepare the royal icing. Use either the homemade recipe above, or make up the royal icing sugar from a pack according to the instructions. It is important to remember to sieve the icing sugar for either method before using.
3. Have a jug of water and kitchen paper to hand, before working. Spread the icing round the top of the cake with a sweeping motion. Occasionally dip the palette knife in the water, wipe dry, and continue to ice the cake. This helps to keep your palette knife clean and to spread the icing evenly.
4. Apply the icing to the sides with the same palette knife, but hold the knife vertically to ensure the marzipan is completely covered. Use a side scraper if a flatter, smoother finish is required.
5. Add some additional icing to the top, and lift the palette knife up and down over the surface to give a rough, peaked texture for a more rustic finish.
6. Allow the icing to dry before adding the decorations.

An easy and quick way to decorate a fruit cake. The icing is applied using a large palette knife to create an even coverage, as well as some natural swirls.

Sweep round the sides, using long strokes to give an even coverage. Then use a small, angled palette knife to create some peaks on the cake surface.

PREPARING ROYAL ICING TO 'FLAT ICE' A CAKE

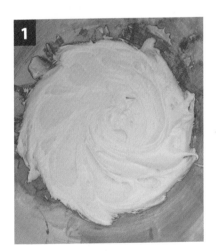

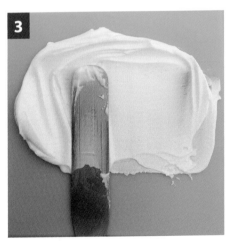

Whichever recipe is used to make royal icing, it is important to remember not to overbeat the mixture. This will result in a fluffy, bubbly icing that will not give a smooth, even coating. When using either a hand or stand mixer, beat on the lowest speed and add the icing sugar to the egg whites gradually.

When the icing is made, wipe down the sides of the bowl and cover with a clean damp cloth, or decant the icing to a clean, lidded plastic container until ready to use. Leaving the icing overnight will allow any bubbles to come to the surface.

Another method to eliminate any bubbles is to 'paddle' the icing on to a clean, grease-free surface before applying it to the cake.

Pearl anniversary cake. This is a traditional coating for a celebration cake.

Anniversary cakes sometimes mimic the original wedding cake, but usually only one tier is required. This cake can be adapted to suit other small celebrations such as a baptism or a landmark birthday, or for a more formal event. Royal icing a cake using this 'flat ice' method takes time and forward planning. Three coats of icing have been used on this cake, and each coating will need to be dry before adding the next coat. Once iced, the cake will keep well and will also withstand a bumpy car ride if travelling to a venue! A round, royal-iced plaque with a number 30, using the 'run-out' method and some royal-iced flowers, complete the decoration.

You will need:

20cm (8in) round fruit cake pre-covered with marzipan using the top and sides method
1kg (2lb) royal icing with added glycerine
30cm (11.8in) cake drum
Large palette knife
Icing ruler
Metal side scraper
Icing turntable
Cake stand (optional)

For the decorations:

Royal icing: 'firm peak' and 'run-out' consistency
White sugar pearls or dragées (optional)
Royal-iced piped flowers
'Pearl' edible dust
Vodka or lemon juice
Piping bags and icing nozzles 1, 2 and 107

Acetate sheet or waxed paper
Vegetable fat or petal base
Masking tape
Mini palette knife
Small paintbrush
Angled desk lamp

Check the consistency of the icing before starting. If it appears a little bubbly, then it will need to be 'rubbed down', as explained before. The first two coats should be 'soft peak'. If the icing has been left to stand for a while, it will need to be stirred gently before using. Always keep the icing covered with a damp cloth to prevent it from crusting when it is not being used.

Add a small dot of royal icing to the centre of the cake drum before placing the marzipan-covered cake on top. Place the cake on a turntable. A small piece of non-slip mat is useful if the turntable does not have a non-slip surface, as this will help anchor the cake whilst you are working.

Using a large palette knife, apply a small amount of icing to the top of the cake in the centre. Use backward and forward strokes keeping the knife flat, as if spreading butter on a slice of bread, then keep the knife in one position and use the turntable to move the cake round until the surface has been completely covered. To even out the surface, hold the tip of the palette knife in the centre of the cake and make a complete turn of the cake using the turntable.

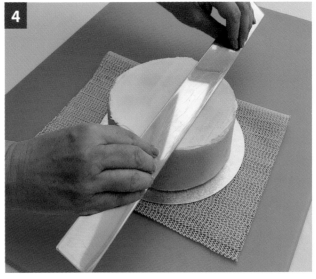

For the next step, move the cake on to a non-slip mat. Wipe the icing ruler with a damp cloth and position it on the far edge of the cake. Hold both ends of the ruler with both hands and at a 10-degree angle to the surface of the cake. Pull the ruler towards you using a quick sweeping action, then pull it off. If there are any flaws, wipe the ruler clean and repeat.

Hold the palette knife parallel with the side of the cake, and using a downward cutting action, remove the surplus icing from the top edge of the cake a small amount at a time, and wiping the knife each time. Leave until dry. The icing will become matte and will feel dry when touched. The time needed will depend on room temperature as well as the thickness of the icing, but is usually several hours.

To coat the sides, hold the palette knife vertically and parallel to the side of the cake, apply small amounts of icing to the bottom edge and use a paddling action to spread these upwards and around the cake.

Wipe the metal side scraper with a damp cloth. Hold the scraper with your fingers spread apart and positioned at a 30-degree angle to the side of the cake. Press gently into the icing and keep in the same position. With the other hand, hold the turntable and then turn through a complete 360-degree turn, and lift away the scraper. The mark left is known as the 'take-off mark' and is unavoidable. If there are any other grooves or flaws in the coating, wipe the scraper clean and repeat.

When the icing is dry, use a sharp knife to scrape away any sharp edges as well as the 'take-off' mark. Remove any sugar dust with a soft dry pastry brush. Repeat steps 3 to 8 to provide a second coat to the cake. Leave to dry. For the final coat add a little more water to the icing to give a softer icing, and coat the top and sides as before. Allow to dry completely.

The cake drum can also be coated with the same icing by paddling small amounts using the tip of a palette knife. Smooth the icing on the board by holding the knife in place at a 10-degree angle, and make a complete turn of the turntable. Allow to dry.

To neaten the base of the cake where it joins the board, use a no. 2 piping tube in a small piping bag and pipe small dots round the base: this is known as a 'snail trail'. 15mm ribbon can be attached to the edge of the cake drum, either by using double-sided sticky tape or a non-toxic glue stick.

Decorating the Cake

The cake is now ready for you to add some decorations to the sides and top. The plaque, numbers and flowers are all made with royal icing. Piping requires plenty of practice as well as a steady hand, so it is worth spending time practising piping lines and curves as well as some piped flowers, before piping on to the cake. Begin by making the plaque as this will need at least 24 hours to dry, before placing on the cake.

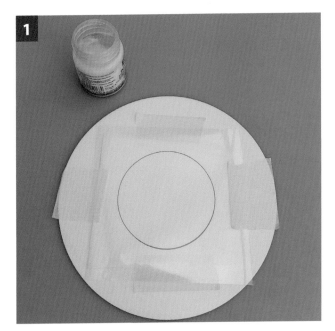

To make the plaque, begin by drawing an 8cm (3in) circle on to some plain paper: this will be the template. Attach the paper to a small work board, either with drawing pins or tape. Place either a piece of acetate sheet or waxed paper (waxed side) that is slightly larger than the circle over the top, and stick down with masking tape or pins. If using acetate, smear a small dot of vegetable fat over the acetate. This will make it easier to remove the iced plaque when dry.

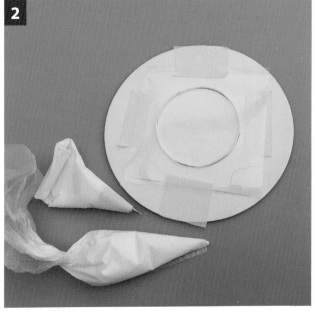

Prepare two piping bags, one medium sized without a nozzle and one smaller bag fitted with a no.1 piping nozzle. Half fill the medium bag with the run-out icing, and fold down the top of the bag tightly. Fill the smaller piping bag, fitted with the no.1 piping nozzle, with firm icing. Use this to pipe over the line on the template. Ensure the joins are neat and just touching each other, but not overlapping.

Snip off the tip of the medium bag of run-out icing and begin to fill the circle, starting round the edges first. Keep the tip of the bag in the icing whilst maintaining a steady pressure. Use the tip of a damp paintbrush to tease out the icing to fill any small gaps. Gently tap the board to level out the icing, and burst any bubbles with the tip of the paintbrush.

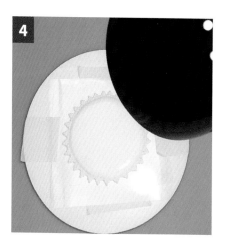

Using the firm icing, pipe tiny dots round the edge of the plaque. Place the plaque under an angle-poised lamp to dry. The warmth of the lamp will give a glossy sheen to the icing, rather than a matte finish. Run-out plaques are quite fragile, so it is a good idea to make two or three in case of breakages.

To make the number 30 decoration, use the same method as above. Again, make some spare numbers in case of breakages. The run-out icing for the numbers can be coloured, or left plain and painted afterwards, as shown here. Mix a little pearl-coloured edible dust with either vodka or lemon juice to make a smooth paint, and use this to colour the numbers. Allow to dry.

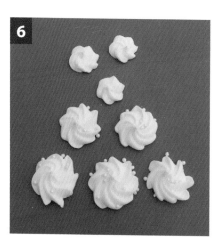

Pipe some simple flowers using a drop nozzle on to an acetate sheet. These will be used to decorate the top edge of the cake. Leave to dry completely before removing them from the acetate sheet.

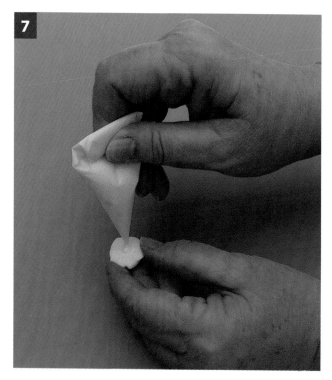

Use a small dot of royal icing under each piped flower, and attach them to the top of the cake as shown.

When both the plaque and the number run-outs are completely dry, use a little soft royal icing to attach the numbers to the centre of the plaque. Do not apply too much pressure as both can easily break. Attach the plaque to the centre of the cake using the same soft icing.

How to Make a Parchment Paper Piping Bag

Cut some triangular sheets of parchment paper. Place the triangle so that the middle point is facing towards you.

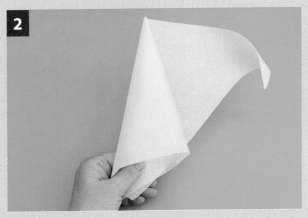

Take one of the top corners and roll it over to meet the bottom point of the triangle to create a cone shape.

Take the remaining top corner and wrap it round the cone so that both the corners and the point are lined up.

Hold the base of the cone and make small adjustments with your fingers to create its sharp point.

Adjust the tightness of the cone and ensure the tip is still at a sharp point. Finally, fold the tails of paper inwards, and then fold inwards again to secure the bag.

Make two cuts in the folded side of the bag and fold in again. This will prevent the bag from unravelling when you are piping.

Snip off the tip of the bag before inserting a piping nozzle. Only fill the bag half full of icing. To seal the bag, fold in the sides first, then fold down the top edge with the seam of the bag at the back.

PASTILLAGE

Pastillage is a type of modelling paste. It is traditionally made with royal icing and gum tragacanth. Its origins date back to the eighteenth century, and it was often used to make rigid decorations on highly ornate royal-iced cakes as it is extremely strong and able to withstand a humid atmosphere. It is an easy modelling paste to make but does dry out very quickly, so any templates and equipment being used need to be ready before making the paste. Numbers, lettering and shapes made with pastillage are useful cake toppers for buttercream cupcakes and larger cakes as they are less affected by moisture. The little gingerbread-house cake topper shown was made using pastillage and decorated with royal icing.

Pastillage is available to buy as a packet mix to be made up with just water, or it can be made very easily at home using egg white, icing sugar and gum tragacanth. Other synthetic gums, such as Tylose powder or CMC, can be used instead of the more expensive gum tragacanth. Below is a simple recipe:

Ingredients:

1 egg white
320g (11½oz) icing sugar, sifted
2tsp gum tragacanth (Tylose or CMC)

Method:

1. Put approximately half the icing sugar into a large mixing bowl and then mix in the egg white until the mixture combines. Then add in the gum tragacanth or other gum powder. Knead into a ball.

2. Place the remaining icing sugar on to a work board or work surface and then turn out the paste on to the icing. Incorporate the icing into the pastillage ball, and knead well until it is a very stiff paste. Not all the icing sugar may be needed.

3. Smooth a little solid vegetable fat over the surface of the ball to prevent it from crusting over, and then double bag into freezer bags.

4. Pastillage will keep in a fridge for up to one month. It will require kneading to warm it up and bring it back to a malleable state before using.

5. To use, roll out small amounts on to a work board dusted with cornflour, and use either cutters or a sharp knife to cut out the required shapes. Allow to dry, then turn the shapes over to dry the other side. When the pieces are completely dry they can be painted with liquid colours or an edible paint made from edible powder colours and clear alcohol, or lemon juice. They can also be dusted with edible powders, including gold and silver dusts.

A gingerbread-house cake topper made using pastillage.

PROJECT 15: SMALL SQUARE CELEBRATION CAKE WITH A COLLAR

Interest in older cake-decorating styles has seen a revival in recent years, and this is a great way to transform a small cake into an elegant and impressive centrepiece. It also has the advantage of making a small cake look much larger. This design is for a small family gathering to celebrate the arrival of a baby boy. The decorations in the centre and round the sides have been pre-made and are available from most cake decorating suppliers.

You will need:

15cm (6in) square cake pre-covered with marzipan using the panel method

500g (17½oz) royal icing with added glycerine

23cm (9in) square cake drum

Large palette knife

Icing ruler

Metal side scraper

Icing turntable

Square cake stand (optional)

Pre-made icing decorations – centre plaque and icing baby feet

A royal-iced cake collar is a classical English decorating technique.

Method for royal icing a square cake:

1. Attach the cake to the cake drum and check the consistency of the icing. As in the previous project, the first two coats should be of 'soft peak' consistency. Remember to keep the icing covered with a damp cloth to prevent the icing from crusting when not being used.

2. Place the cake on to a turntable. Use a large palette knife to apply a small amount of icing to the top of the cake in the centre. Ensure the tip of the knife runs centrally along the top of the cake, and paddle the icing.

3. Turn the cake round 90 degrees on the turntable and repeat the paddling. Continue adding icing and paddling until the top is covered.

4. For the next step, move the cake on to a non-slip mat. Wipe the icing ruler with a damp cloth and position it on the far edge of the cake. Hold both ends of the ruler with both hands and at a 10-degree angle to the surface of the cake. Pull the ruler towards you, using a quick sweeping action, and then pull it off. If there are any flaws, wipe the ruler clean and repeat.

5. Position the cake back on to the turntable. Hold the palette knife parallel with the side of the cake, and using a downward-cutting action, remove the surplus icing from the top edge of the cake a small amount at a time and wiping the knife each time. Leave until dry. The icing will become matte and feel dry when touched. The time needed will depend on room temperature as well as the thickness of the icing, but this usually takes at least eight hours.

6. When coating a square cake, the two opposite sides must be coated first and allowed to dry, before coating the remaining two sides. This will ensure the cake has sharp edges. Hold the palette knife vertically and parallel to the side of the cake, apply small amounts of icing to the bottom edge, and use a paddling action to work the icing up to the top edge until the whole side is covered.

7. Wipe the metal side scraper with a damp cloth. Hold the scraper with fingers spread apart, and position at a 30-degree angle to the side of the cake. Press gently into the icing, and with one action, pull the scraper across the side of the cake. If there are any other grooves or flaws in the coating, wipe the scraper clean and repeat.

8. Once a smooth side is achieved, clean off the top and side edges with the palette knife, as described in the previous project instructions for the round cake. Repeat on the opposite side of the cake and leave to dry before coating the two remaining sides.

9. Repeat steps 6 to 8 to provide a second coat to the cake. For the final coat, add a little more water to the icing to give a softer icing, and coat the top and sides as before. Allow to dry completely.

10. If using a plain cake drum, icing can be applied for a neat finish. To coat the cake drum, apply the icing with a palette knife and paddle until the board is completely covered.

11. Hold the edge of the scraper level with the cake drum and pull it along the cake drum in one smooth action. Repeat for the three remaining sides.

12. Remove the excess icing from the edges of the drum using a downward cutting action with the palette knife. Carefully wipe clean the edges with a damp cloth as it will be difficult to attach a ribbon if any icing is remaining on the drum edges.

13. Allow the cake to dry completely before either piping a 'snail trail', or attaching a ribbon round the base of the cake. Ribbon can also be used round the cake-drum edge.

Coat the two opposite sides of a square cake first.

Making a Royal Icing Collar

Begin by taking accurate measurements of the finished cake. The overall finished size of the cake with the collar must not be larger than the cake drum. The inside collar measurement must be smaller than the top of the cake, so that the collar can be attached securely. Using a set square will ensure the inside edge of the collar will have 90-degree corners, and a compass will help to draw curved shapes for the outside edges.

What you need for the icing collar and other decorations:

Royal icing: 'firm peak' and 'run-out' consistency

Food colouring

Piping bags and icing nozzle 1

Acetate sheet or waxed paper

Vegetable fat or petal base

Masking tape

Ruler

Mini palette knife

Small paintbrush

Angled desk lamp

Set square and compass

Royal-iced decorations (culpitt decorations have been used in this project)

Pre-made plaque using a small quantity of pastillage and embossing stamp (laser cut)

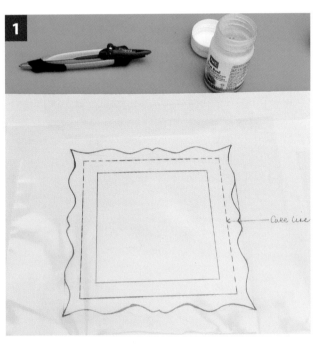

Draw a plan for the cake collar. The red dotted line indicates the actual size of the cake. Attach the template to a small work board, either with drawing pins or tape. Then place over the top of it either a piece of acetate sheet or waxed paper (waxed side) that is slightly larger than the template, and stick it down with masking tape or pins. If using acetate, smear a small dot of vegetable fat over the acetate; this will make it easier to remove the iced collar when dry.

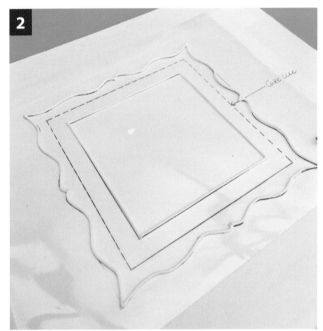

Using a piping bag with a no.1 nozzle, pipe over the outlines of the design.

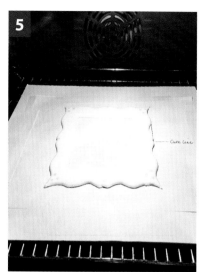

Soften some icing to 'run out' consistency. The thickness should be similar to single cream and when a knife is drawn across the surface of the icing, the line should disappear by a count of five. Pour the icing slowly into a piping bag: pouring it down the side of the bag will help eliminate any bubbles. Prepare another bag of blue run-out icing.

Cut a no. 2 nozzle-sized hole in the tip of the bag, and use it to flood the collar. Flood in small areas at a time. Then pipe some blue dots on to the colour whilst the white icing is still wet.

Place the collar either under a desk lamp or into an oven with no heat but just the oven light on until the surface crusts over. Remove and allow to dry out completely somewhere warm and dry. When the collar has dried completely, use a small palette knife to release the collar from the acetate or paper.

Final Decorations

Allow the cake to dry completely before attaching the plaque to the centre of the cake and the icing 'feet' to the sides using dots of soft icing. Attach some ribbon to the board, using either a non-toxic glue stick or double-sided tape.

Pipe a line of softened royal icing along the top edges of the cake and carefully place the collar into position. Do not press down. Allow to dry. Attach decorations on the top and the sides of the cake with some dots of royal icing.

CHAPTER 8

SUGARPASTE

· · · · · · · · · · ·

Sugarpaste, also known as 'fondant icing' and 'ready to roll' icing, has become extremely popular in recent years with most professional and home-based cake decorators. It can be used to cover any type of cake and is easy to apply. It gives a smooth, polished finish that will firm up when dry, but still remain soft enough to cut easily.

While the paste is still soft it can be textured and embossed, and when dry it provides a good base for piping on with royal icing. Sugarpaste can also be used for modelling figures and shapes. The paste can be made firmer by adding either gum tragacanth or a synthetic gum powder, such as CMC or Tylose. It is also the perfect medium for using with metal flower cutters and plunger cutters.

Sugarpaste is readily available in most supermarkets. It is usually called 'ready to roll' icing and sold in either 500g (17½oz) or 1kg (2lb) blocks as well as in ready rolled sheets. Specialist cake-decorating suppliers sell a number of different brands in larger quantities as well as in a variety of colours.

Homemade Sugarpaste

Although it is a more expensive option to make sugarpaste rather than buying it ready-made, it is an easy icing to make at home. This recipe yields enough sugarpaste to cover a 20cm (8in) cake.

Ingredients:
60ml (2fl oz) cold water
4tsp powdered gelatine
125ml (4fl oz) liquid glucose
15ml (½fl oz) glycerine
1kg (2lb) icing sugar, sieved, plus extra for dusting

Method:
1. Place the water in a small bowl and sprinkle over the gelatine. When the gelatine has turned to a jelly, place the bowl over a pan of gently simmering water and stir until the gelatine has dissolved. Add the glucose and glycerine, continue to stir until the mixture is runny.
2. Put the icing sugar into a large bowl and make a well in the centre, then slowly pour in the liquid ingredients, stirring constantly. Continue to mix until the liquid is incorporated, then turn out on to a surface dusted with icing sugar and knead until smooth. If the paste becomes too sticky, dust over some of the reserved icing sugar.
3. The paste is ready to use immediately. It can be stored for later use or frozen for up to three months. Double wrap in freezer bags and remove as much air as possible from the bag.

PROJECT 16: DAISY RING CELEBRATION CAKE

Daisy ring celebration cake.

This would be an ideal cake for a summer birthday celebration. The flowers are made using plunger cutters, which are readily available to buy online or from cake and craft shops. The sugarpaste has been coloured using edible paste colours in this project, but pre-coloured sugarpaste could also be used. This project explains how to cover a crumb coated buttercream cake with sugarpaste. The same method is also used when covering a ganache- or marzipan-coated cake. The marzipan will need to be moistened before coating with sugarpaste by brushing lightly over it with either clear alcohol, such as vodka, or cooled boiled water.

Ingredients:

For the cake covering:

20cm (8in) round cake, crumb coated with buttercream (refer to Project 2)

25cm (10in) cake drum

900g (32oz) white sugarpaste + 100g (3½oz) for decorations

Cornflour or icing sugar for dusting

Rolling pin

Non-stick board

Plastic bag

Smoother(s)

Scriber/glass-headed pin

Small sharp knife

Spacers or rolling-pin guides

Turntable

Ruler or tape measure

For the decoration:

Edible paste colours – yellow, green, black

Daisy plunger cutter set (PME or cake star)

Alphabet cutters (FMM)

Ribbon

Modelling tools – ball tool, Dresden tool (FMM)

Stay-fresh mat

Solid vegetable fat (Trex or PME petal base)

Edible glue or small quantity of royal icing

Gum tragacanth or CMC/tylose

Method for covering the cake:

First prepare the cake by filling, crumb coating and then attaching it to the cake drum as described in Project 2. Place in the fridge to chill for 30 minutes. This will set the buttercream and make it easier to sugarpaste.

Measure the top and sides of the cake to calculate how large the sugarpaste will need to be when rolled out. If using a 20cm (8in) cake that is 7.5cm (3in) deep, the icing will need to measure 35cm (14in) across. Knead the sugarpaste on a non-stick board until it is soft and pliable.

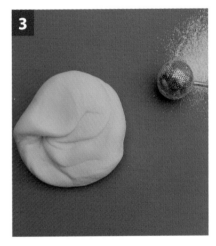

If working on a non-stick surface, cornflour or icing sugar may not be needed, but have a little amount to hand if the paste becomes tacky. Using too much can cause the paste to dry out and crack, making it difficult to work with. It can also take on the appearance of what is commonly known as 'elephant skin'.

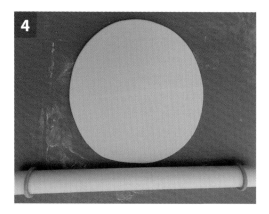

Use a non-stick rolling pin to roll out the paste, gently lifting and frequently turning it when rolling. This will prevent the paste from sticking and will help to keep it in a circular shape. The paste needs to be approximately 5mm (0.2in) thick. Using spacers on each side of the paste, or some rolling-pin guides as shown, will help ensure an even thickness.

When the icing is rolled out to the correct size, flip it on to the rolling pin towards you. Place it against the front side of the cake and lay the paste over the cake, moving the rolling pin away from you as the paste is unrolled over the cake. This action reduces the possibility of trapping air under the paste, causing air bubbles.

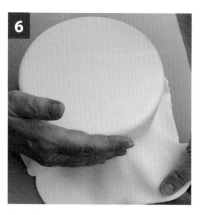

Smooth the top with your hand, then work round the sides lifting out any pleats. Do not be tempted to squash pleats or creases into the cake. Work gradually round the sides of the cake, gently lifting out any creases with one hand and smoothing down with the other.

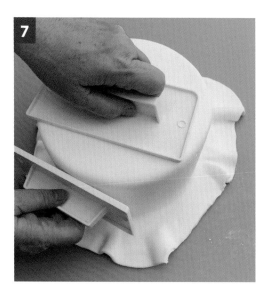

Smooth and polish the surface and sides with a smoother. Use two smoothers, one in each hand, to give an even surface without any finger marks.

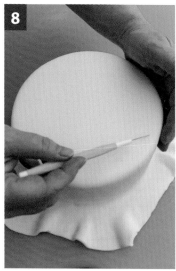

Remove any air bubbles with a scribing tool or glass-headed pin, by pricking a tiny hole in the centre of the air bubble and rubbing it over with the smoother in a circular motion, easing the air out and sealing the hole.

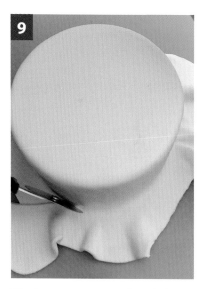

Trim the excess sugarpaste from the base of the cake using either a sharp knife or a pizza-wheel cutter, and smooth any rough edges with the straight edge of the smoother. Place the excess paste into a plastic freezer-type bag. (Avoid using clingfilm as it is not completely air tight.)

Method for covering the board using 'the bandage' method:

To cover the board, roll a sausage of sugarpaste the same length as the outside diameter of the board. Dust the work surface with a little icing sugar, and roll out into a strip 5mm (0.2in) thick and approximately the width of the board.

Trim one side of the strip with a sharp knife to create a straight edge. Dust the strip with a little cornflour or icing sugar, and gently roll up the paste strip like a bandage.

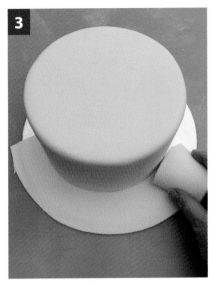

Brush a little cooled boiled water on to the cake board before carefully unrolling the sugarpaste 'bandage' round the cake. Gently push the cut side of the paste strip up to the base of the cake when unrolling.

Overlap the join and cut through both strips. Remove the excess flap of paste and smooth over the join with the cake smoother.

Trim the excess paste from the board edge with a sharp knife. Smooth the edge of the board using the side of your hand.

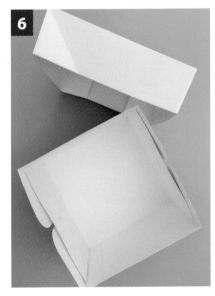

Place the cake in a cardboard cake box in a cool, dry room overnight. Do not place it in the fridge or use a plastic container as this will cause the paste to 'sweat' and become sticky.

Decorating the cake:

Using a ball tool, gently mark the position of the flowers on the surface of the cake. Although the paste will now be firm, it will still be soft enough to make an impression.

Make some modelling paste by adding ¼tsp of gum tragacanth or CMC powder to 100g (3½oz) sugarpaste. Knead the paste well until the powder is fully incorporated. Wrap in a plastic bag and leave to stiffen for about 30 minutes.

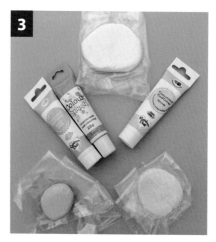

Take half the modelling paste and place the remainder back in the plastic bag to prevent it drying out. Divide this in half again and colour one part yellow and the other green. Further shades can also be made. Place the coloured pastes into plastic bags.

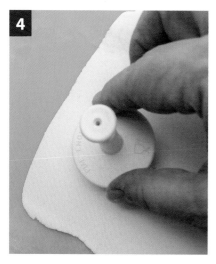

Lightly grease one side of a non-stick work board with vegetable fat and dust the other side with cornflour. Roll out some of the white modelling paste very thinly on to the greased side of the board, then transfer the paste on to the floured side. Using the largest daisy cutter in the set, press down holding only the sides of the cutter, and move the cutter in a circular motion to cut through the paste.

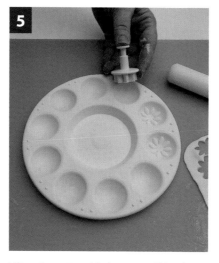

Lift up the cutter with the paste still inside, and press the plunger to release the flower. Allow to dry in a paint palette that has a curved base. This will give the flowers a '3d' shape. Once dry, attach the flowers with a small dot of royal icing.

Continue adding more flowers, using different sizes of cutter. To make the daisy centres, roll tiny balls of yellow paste and attach them to the flower centres with either edible glue or royal icing. Use the green modelling paste to make some leaves. The leaves can be attached to the cake immediately or allowed to dry first.

Further modelling paste decorations can be added, such as butterflies or bees. Plunger butterfly cutters have been used here. They are made in the same way as the flowers, but have been dried on folded cardboard as shown.

Yellow modelling paste has been used for the lettering. Roll out a long strip of paste on the cornflour-dusted surface and leave until touch dry. Dust the cutter with cornflour before placing it across the strip of paste. Press down, rub it from side to side to achieve a clean cut, and then tap the cutter on the work surface to release the letter. Use a paintbrush with either edible glue or water to attach the letters to the cake surface.

To complete the cake decoration, attach a 15mm (0.6in)-width ribbon to the base of the cake and the edge of the cake drum, using double-sided tape.

Trouble-Shooting Tips for Sugarpaste

Sugarpaste is too hard to roll out: If this is a new pack, place it in the microwave for five seconds and then knead well. Sugarpaste dries out very quickly, so avoid leaving it uncovered.

Sugarpaste has cracks in it: This is sometimes due to the paste not being kneaded enough before rolling it out. Use either your hands or a cake smoother and gently rub the paste with a circular motion until the cracks disappear. This will only work when the paste is still soft.

Sugarpaste has a tear: Bring the two pieces of sugarpaste back together by gently pushing each side of the tear. Then use the above method of smoothing gently in circular motions to lessen the crack. If there is still a visible line, a strategically placed decoration could be used to cover the join.

Sugarpaste is too dry and looks like elephant skin: Usually this is a result of using too much icing sugar or cornflour when rolling out. Try kneading in a small amount of vegetable fat such as Trex.

Sugarpaste is sticky: This happens if the paste has come into contact with water, or it has been stored in a plastic container. If the finished cake is sticky, this is due to storing it in the fridge or a plastic container, which is the incorrect thing to do. Avoid touching the cake surface, and place the cake in a cardboard cake box at room temperature and it will dry out.

There are air bubbles in the paste: Use a clean pin or scribing tool to pop each bubble and gently smooth the surface with your hand or a cake smoother.

FONDANT ICING

Fondant icing in the UK is a thick, pourable icing, known best as the coating on the popular tea-time treat, fondant fancies. Fondant icing contains the same ingredients as sugarpaste, of icing sugar, liquid glucose, glycerine and water, but the consistencies of the two icings differ due to the different quantities of the ingredients.

Fondant icing is readily available as a packet mix in most supermarkets. As well as being used as a coating icing, it can also be made into the stiff paste known as sugarpaste, for covering a cake. If used in this way add four to five teaspoons of water to 250g (9oz) of fondant icing sugar. Knead well and then follow the method above for using sugarpaste.

Fondant fancies are a popular teatime treat.

Fondant fancies are a quintessential tea-time favourite and popular with all ages. They are time-consuming to make, but the sponges and filling can be made in advance and frozen for up to three months, leaving only the coating of icing to be done on the day. To make the fondant icing in this project, a block of sugarpaste has been used instead of the fondant mix. It is more easily available to buy in the supermarket, and demonstrates its versatility as a cake covering. Alternatively use a 1kg (2lb) pack of fondant icing sugar.

Ingredients:

For the cake:
200g (7oz) butter, softened
200g (7oz) caster sugar
1tsp vanilla extract
4 eggs, medium
200g (7oz) self-raising flour

For the filling:
150g (5½oz) raspberry jam
100g (3½oz) butter, softened
125g (4½oz) icing sugar

For the covering:
3tbsp apricot jam
500g (17½oz) marzipan

For the icing:
1kg (2lb) white fondant icing
150ml (5fl oz) water
Pink gel food colouring
Yellow gel food colouring

Method for making the sponges:

1. Preheat the oven to 180°C/160°C fan/gas mark 4. Grease and line a 20cm (8in) square tin with baking parchment.

2. Cream together the butter and sugar until light and fluffy using either a stand mixer or a hand whisk.

3. Add the vanilla extract and then the eggs, one at a time, mixing well between each addition. Add a little flour if the mixture starts to curdle.

4. Fold in the flour, using a spatula or large metal spoon until fully incorporated into the mixture.

5. Spread the mixture into the prepared tin and bake for 30–40 minutes or until a skewer inserted comes out clean. Allow the cake to cool in the tin for ten minutes, before turning out on to a wire rack to cool completely.

6. To make the buttercream, beat the softened butter with the icing sugar using an electric whisk until light and fluffy.

7. Prepare the cake by slicing off the surface if it has domed, before slicing the cake in half. Spread a thin layer of buttercream over one half of the cake. Reserve the remaining buttercream for later.

8. Spread the raspberry jam over the other half and then sandwich the cake together. Wrap well and chill in the fridge for 30 minutes. This will make it easier to cut the cakes into squares.

9. Remove the cake from the fridge. Trim the sides of the cake to neaten, and then use a ruler and a serrated knife to cut the cake into quarters and then into quarters again to give sixteen small cakes.

10. At this point the cakes can be frozen, ready to be iced at a future date. If continuing with the recipe, then chill the cakes in the fridge whilst rolling out the marzipan.

Decorating the fondant fancies:

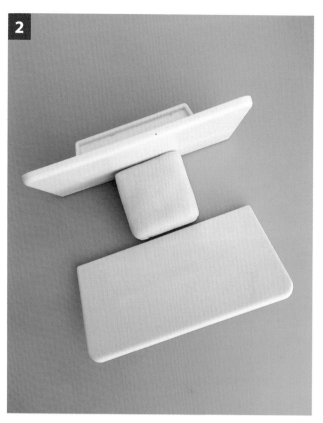

Prepare the marzipan by rolling it out thinly and then cut 16 x 12cm (6.3 x 4.7in) circles using a pastry cutter. Remove one cake from the fridge and check that the size of the marzipan circle is large enough to cover the cakes. Adjust as needed, then brush the top and sides of each cake with apricot glaze before covering with marzipan. Use scissors to trim away the excess paste along the sides and the bottom edges.

Use two cake smoothers to push the cake into a more uniform cube shape.

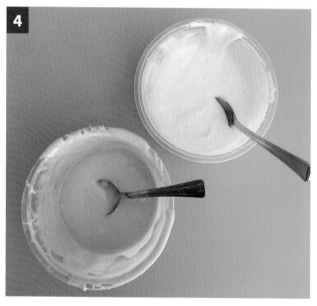

To make the icing, break the fondant into small pieces and place into the bowl of a stand mixer with the paddle attachment. With the mixer on a low speed, gradually add the water, mixing until the fondant begins to break down and the icing becomes smooth and pourable.

Put 2tbsp of the icing into a piping bag to use as decoration later, and divide the remaining mixture into two bowls. Colour one with pink food colouring and the other with yellow.

Remove the cakes from the fridge and place on a wire rack with a sheet of baking parchment underneath. Spoon the icing over the cakes to cover them, then leave to set at room temperature for 30 minutes.

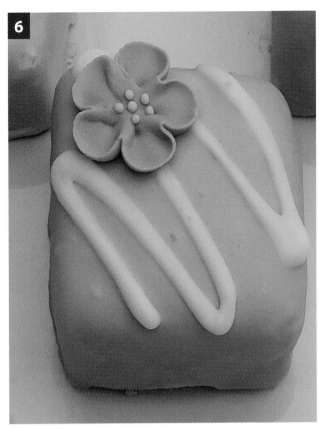

Pipe the reserved white icing over the top of the cakes in a zigzag pattern. Attach some small sugar flowers, then allow the cakes to set completely at room temperature.

COLOURING SUGARPASTE AND CREATING PATTERNS

Colouring sugarpaste is very easy to do, but it is important to use a concentrated gel colouring paste rather than a liquid colouring as this will not affect the consistency of the sugarpaste quite as much. If the paste becomes too sticky, dust your hands with a little cornflour.

Continue to add a little more colour if the shade achieved is not deep enough. However, the paste will deepen in colour if left for a few hours. Ensure the paste is well wrapped in a plastic bag, to avoid drying out.

When colouring large quantities, it is easier to colour a small quantity of paste to a deep shade and then add the coloured paste to the remaining white paste. Pre-coloured paste can also be used in this way.

Very dark or strong colours, such as red or black, are difficult to achieve using this method, so it is recommended to buy the sugarpaste pre-coloured.

Colouring sugarpaste and creating patterns.

Begin by kneading the sugarpaste until it is smooth and stretchy, then apply a very small amount of gel colour, using a cocktail stick.

A marbled effect is achieved by half blending colours together. This technique has been used in Project 18.

TEXTURING, EMBOSSING AND INLAY TECHNIQUES

Some of the following techniques originate from other crafts, such as needle and leatherwork.

Broderie anglaise is a technique used to decorate linen tablecloths and napkins. These cutters mimic the design in sugarpaste.

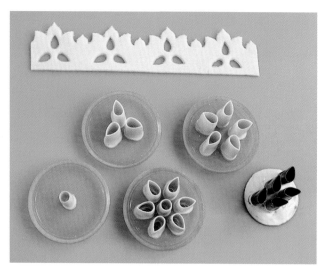

Broderie anglaise eyelet cutters are available to use with modelling paste.

Sugarpaste can be textured easily, either by using textured silicone mats or rolling pins. Begin by rolling out the quantity of paste required on a cornflour-dusted work surface.

To use a textured rolling pin, roll out the sugarpaste as before using a plain rolling pin, then roll over the paste again using the textured pin.

To use a textured mat, dust with cornflour, then lay the mat on top of the sugarpaste. Roll over the mat using a firm, even pressure.

Lightly dusting both the paste surface and the rolling pin with a little cornflour will prevent sticking.

Dust the paste, cutter or embossing tool with cornflour and gently press into the paste to imprint it.

Embossing sugarpaste can be done by using flower cutters and shapes as well as embossing tools, specifically made for sugarcraft.

Patterns can also be created by inlaying pieces of sugarpaste into the base layer. This technique can be used to create patterns with different coloured pastes. Begin as before, by rolling out the background sugarpaste and then covering it with either a stay-fresh mat or a plastic bag to prevent it from drying out whilst preparing the shapes to be applied. Use any small flower cutters or shape cutters such as stars or holly leaves, as shown. Remove the plastic mat from the background paste and place the shapes on the top. Roll over the paste once in one direction and then

roll again in the opposite direction: this will minimise any distortion of the shapes.

Other side designs on cakes, such as using moulds to create texture as well as a 3D effect, are usually made with modelling paste. This is a 50/50 mix of sugarpaste and flowerpaste (also called gumpaste). Flowerpaste is a stiff modelling paste, mainly used for creating sugar flowers. This mix gives a stronger and stretchier paste to work with. This paste is also used for a technique called pleating, sometimes known as Japanese pleating (see box).

Modelling paste is also useful for creating rope borders, ruffles, frills, billows and bows. These can be used as decorations for the sides and top of a cake as well as providing a decorative edging. Some of these techniques can be found in Chapter 9 'Finishing Touches.'

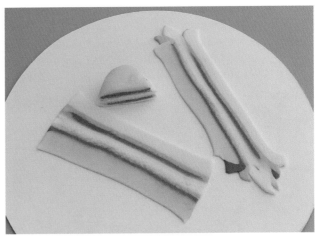

To create a striped paste, different coloured pastes are rolled out very thinly and laid on top of one another before being cut, turned on its side and then gently rolled to fuse the pastes together.

Apply the shapes whilst the sugarpaste is still soft.

Japanese pleating is a popular decorating technique on larger, tiered cakes.

Japanese Pleating

This technique can be used on either a single cake or as one of the tiers in a multi-tiered cake. It requires a cake already sugarpasted to work on, as well as some modelling paste to create the pleats.

Before making the pleats, use a scribing tool to mark the size of the above tier into the top of the cake. This is the guide for how far on top of the cake the pleats are to sit, as these pleats will not cover the top of the cake.

Place the sugarpasted cake on a small stand as it needs to be elevated so that when the pleats are attached to the cake, the bottom can be folded under the cake base. A large ramekin has been used here.

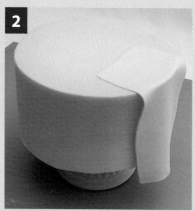

Roll out a very thin piece of 50:50 SFP/ sugarpaste. Measure the height of the cake and add a few centimetres to the length, giving enough to fold over the top of the cake and underneath.

Lay the paste over three greased skewers or dowels. Smooth over the dowels to create grooves in between. Fold in the edges of the paste to create a seam. This will give a neat edge to each panel.

Pinch the top and bottom of the paste to create the pleats. Brush a section of the cake with edible glue or water, including the top and bottom edges, and then carefully attach the paste to the top of the cake.

Fold the bottom of the paste underneath and press firmly to attach it. Brush the side of the attached panel before adding the next. Continue round the cake until all the panels are attached.

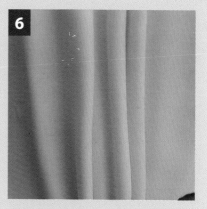

Once all the pleats are attached, place the cake on a cake board or flat surface to dry. This will ensure the base of the cake dries flat.

A three-tier
wedding cake.

A wedding cake is probably regarded by most as the ultimate show stopper cake. A cake with three tiers is one of the most popular sizes for a wedding cake, but this is dependent on several factors, such as the number of servings required, the type of cake used, and the overall cost of the cake. Although a rich fruit cake is a traditional choice for a wedding cake, it is now more popular to have a different type of cake for each layer.

Whichever cakes are chosen, the most important consideration when constructing a tiered cake is stability. This is achieved by knowing how to prepare a stacked cake correctly, by having the correct equipment and ingredients, and allowing plenty of time to prepare and build the cake.

Before making the cake, consider the design, colour scheme and the type of decoration required. Traditionally, there are flowers on the cake. These can be either fresh, silk or handmade sugar flowers. Colours are usually chosen to compliment the bridal bouquet and other floral decorations. The cake itself can also be covered with a coloured icing, although a white or ivory coating remains the most popular choice. In this project I have used different design elements for each tier, but these are merely examples of different techniques that can be applied.

Stacking a cake needs an internal structure that will support the weight of the cakes. This is done by inserting dowels and using thin cake boards under each cake.

The instructions for dowelling and stacking the tiers can also be used for any number of tiers, different shaped cakes, and alternative cake coverings. The method is the same. When stacking more than three tiers, or if the cake is being transported to a venue and extra stability is required, an additional middle dowel running through all the tiers can be used.

Round cakes have been used in this project. The top tier cake is 15cm (6in), the middle cake is 20cm (8in) and the base cake is 25cm (10in). All the cakes are 13cm (5in) tall.

If sponge cakes are being used, split and fill them, then attach the thin cake boards using a small amount of either buttercream or ganache before crumb coating them with the remaining buttercream or ganache, as described in Project 2, Chapter 3. Alternatively, if using fruit cakes, attach these to the cake boards with a smear of apricot jam before covering them with marzipan using the panel method as described in Project 4, Chapter 4.

You will need:
For the top tier:
1 round 15cm (6in) prepared cake (crumb coated or marzipanned)
1 round 15cm (6in) cake board
500g (17½oz) white sugarpaste
Royal icing
Cake border stencil
Pearl-headed dressmaking pins or masking tape
15mm (0.6in) ribbon
Double-sided sticky tape

For the middle tier:
1 round 20cm (8in) prepared cake
1 round 20cm (8in) cake board
800g (28oz) sugarpaste coloured dusky pink (Sugarflair spectral paste dusky pink)
Lustre dust (Sugarflair shimmer pink)
15mm (0.6in) ribbon
Double-sided sticky tape

For the bottom tier:
1 round 25cm (10in) prepared cake
1 round 25cm (10in) cake board
1kg (2lb) sugarpaste white
300g sugarpaste dusky pink } 1.3kg (3lb)
15mm (0.6in) ribbon
Double-sided sticky tape

For the cake board:
30cm (12in) round cake drum
700g (25oz) sugarpaste white (optional if using a pre-coloured cake drum)
15mm (0.6in) ribbon
Double-sided sticky tape or non-toxic glue stick

Additional tools and equipment:
2 dowels (PME easycut dowels, 30cm (12in))
Royal icing (stencil work and attaching tiers)
Silk flowers (Ivmay Creations)
3 posy pics (PME)
3 cardboard cake boxes (20cm (8in), 25cm (10in) and 30cm (12in)) for storing individual cakes, before stacking)
Baking paper
Serrated bread knife or clean garden shears, for cutting the dowels
Edible ink pen

Method for sugarpasting the cakes:
Covering the board:

Begin by covering the cake board, which is the 30cm (12in) cake drum. This will allow the paste more time to dry out completely, and the cake can be stored in the largest cake box until ready for stacking the cakes. This method covers the drum completely, giving the cake a stable base.

How to make sharp edges on sugarpaste-coated cakes:

If using a marzipan-covered cake, brush the surface with either vodka or cooled boiled water before attaching the sugarpaste. If using a buttercreamed cake, refrigerate for fifteen minutes before attaching the sugarpaste. If using a ganached cake, brush with cooled boiled water.

Measure the dimensions of the cake to calculate how large the sugarpaste covering needs to be. The smallest cake is 15cm (6in) across and 10cm (4in) deep, so the paste will need to be rolled out 35cm (14in) across (15cm + 10cm +10cm = 35cm). For the medium, middle-tier cake

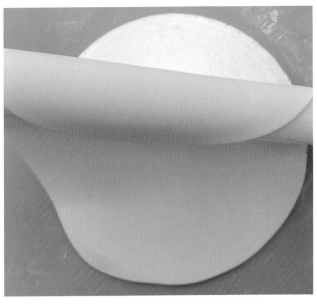

Dampen the cake drum with a piece of moist kitchen roll. Use the rolling pin to lift the sugarpaste and lay it on the board. Use a cake smoother to secure the paste to the board, then use a sharp knife to cut away the excess paste. Wipe the side of the drum to remove remnants of paste. Use the side of your hand to smooth out the cut edge of the paste to give a neat finish. Allow the paste to dry before attaching the ribbon with either double-sided tape or non-toxic glue.

measuring 20cm (8in) across with a depth of 10cm (4in), the covering will need to be rolled out to 40cm (16in) across. The bottom 25cm (10in) cake, with a 10cm (4in) depth, will require the paste to be rolled out 45cm (18in) across.

Cover the cakes with sugarpaste following the instructions in Project 16, earlier in this chapter. Then whilst the paste is still soft, create a sharp edge using one of the following methods.

Method 1: Using flexible smoothers

For this method a set of two flexi-smoothers is needed. The sets are available in three sizes. The medium set is required for the top and medium tier cakes and the large set for the bottom tier. They are available from most cake and

Knead the paste well until it is smooth and stretchy before rolling it out, then lightly dust the work surface with cornflour. Turn and lift the sugarpaste between rolls to keep the shape round and prevent the paste sticking to the board. The paste should have a depth of 5mm (0.2in). Using rolling-pin guides or spacers will help to roll the correct thickness.

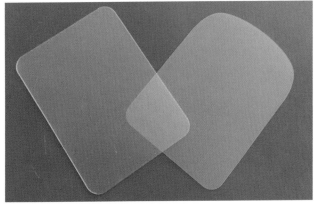

The set used here are called 'Bellisimo Flexi smoothers'.

Move both smoothers round the cake to create a sharp edge.

Using the cake smoother horizontally, gently smooth the cake in a downwards motion. This will draw the paste downwards to make contact with the board.

craft shops as well as online. Other brands are also readily available. One side of the smoother has a smooth surface to use against the cake, and the other side has a slightly rough surface, making them easier to grip.

Hold the straight-edged smoother against the top side of the cake and the curved smoother firmly on top of the cake with the curved edge against the curve of the cake. Hold the curved top smoother still and rub the side smoother against the side of the cake to create a sharp edge.

Method 2: Upside-down method

For this method, a spare cake board covered with non-stick baking parchment is required as well as some cornflour. Whilst the sugarpaste on the cake is still soft, lightly dust the surface with a little cornflour and place the spare cake board on the top. Invert the cake so the top of the cake is at the bottom. Continue until the sides are completely even and the paste is touching the base board all the way round. Turn the cake back over and remove the spare board.

Method 3: Panel method

To attach the sugarpaste in two sections, use the panel method. Follow the instructions for covering a cake with marzipan in Project 5, Chapter 4. This is where the top of the cake is covered first, before adding a roll of paste to the sides. This method will create a sharp edge. Once the paste is applied, use the cake smoother to 'rub out' the joining mark around the top edge of the cake.

In this project, the smallest, top-tier cake is covered in white icing and does not need any dowels inserting. Once this cake has been sugarpasted it can be placed in the 20cm (8in) cake box and allowed to dry before being decorated later.

Colouring the sugarpaste for the middle tier:

The middle tier is covered in a dusky pink-coloured paste. An edible paste colour has been used, which is an extremely concentrated colour and needs to be applied sparingly using the tip of a cocktail stick or toothpick.

Use a folding in and stretching out action to incorporate the colour. Continue to add more dots of paste colour until the depth of shade required is achieved.

Make a paint using the lustre dust and a little of the dipping solution. Use a wide brush to apply the paint as shown.

Wrap the paste completely in a freezer type plastic bag until ready to use. Be aware that the colour will continue to deepen once mixed. 1.1kg (2½lb) of coloured paste is required for this project – 800g (28oz) for the middle tier cake, and 300g (10oz) of this colour will be added to 1kg (2lb) of white paste for the marbled effect on the bottom tier.

When ready to ice the middle tier, use the same method for covering as described for the top tier. This tier can be left plain pink, or given a sheen finish using a lustre dust and some dipping solution.

The paint will dry quickly; if it appears patchy, then apply another coat. When the paint has completely dried, use a large dusting brush to buff the paint, removing any patchy areas to leave a light sheen to the cake.

How to create a marbled effect with sugarpaste:

The bottom tier cake in this project is covered in marbled sugarpaste. Begin by kneading 1kg (2lb) of white sugarpaste until it is smooth and stretchy. Place in a plastic bag whilst kneading 300g (10oz) pink paste. To create a third shade mix some of the white paste with the pink. Additional shades can also be made.

Take the white paste and roll it into a thick sausage. Do the same with the pink paste, then lay the sausage-shaped pastes side by side. Gather the pastes together and twist into an 'S' shape.

Roll out the paste on the work surface. If more marbling is required, roll the paste back up into a sausage, re-twist and re-roll. Avoid overworking the paste too many times as it will begin to dry out and may crack. Cover the cake as described above.

DOWELLING THE CAKES

Once all the cakes have been sugarpasted, dowels need to be inserted into the middle and bottom tier cakes. This is easier to do whilst the sugarpaste is still slightly soft.

To dowel the cakes, begin by marking the top of the bottom tier with either a spare 20cm (8in) cake card or the base of a 20cm (8in) cake tin. Place it in the middle of the

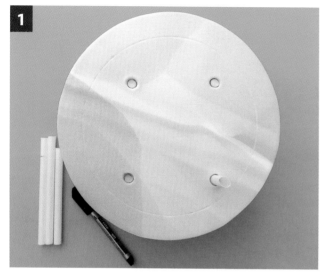

This mark will act as a guide for positioning the middle-tier cake as well as showing the area where the dowels will go.

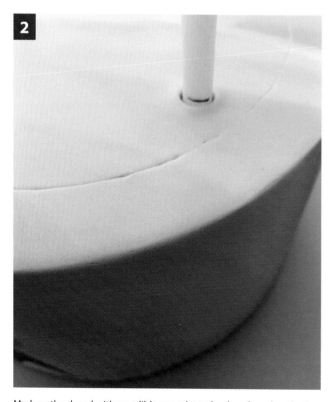

Mark on the dowel with an edible pen where the dowel reaches the top of the cake.

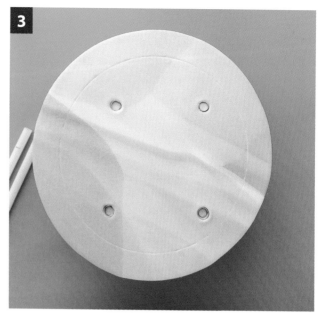

Push the remaining dowels, cut side up, into the cake. Space them evenly within the marked circle.

cake, and either make a slight impression or use a scribing tool to make a mark.

Four dowels are used in the bottom tier and three in the middle tier. Take one of the dowels and push it all the way down into the cake, within the marked circle, until it touches the bottom. Mark with an edible pen.

Remove the dowel by twisting and pulling it out gently. Use either a sharp knife or clean secateurs to cut the dowel at the mark line. Cut the three remaining dowels to the same length using the first dowel as a guide.

Dowel the middle tier cake in the same way. Mark the surface with a 15cm (6in) cake card or the base of a tin, and use three dowels, placed in a triangular position.

The cakes can now be stored in cake boxes before stacking.

DECORATING THE TOP TIER CAKE USING A STENCIL

A border cake stencil has been used in this project. Cake stencils are available to buy from cake-decorating suppliers and craft shops as well as online. Here, royal icing has been used to cover the stencil, but the pattern can also be applied by using powdered edible colours with a brush or by using an airbrush.

The sugarpaste on the cake must be completely dry and hard before stencilling, so it does not dent when adding any pressure to the cake.

Begin by securing the stencil to the cake. This can be done using a few different methods. The simplest is to use either dressmaker's pins or cocktail sticks on either side of the stencil. An alternative method, to avoid pin marks and placing pins directly into the cake, is to extend the length of the stencil. Cut a strip of white paper and attach to one side of the stencil using masking tape.

Use more masking tape to secure the other side of the stencil to the paper strip.

Another method for attaching the stencil to the cake is to apply a very thin layer of vegetable fat (Trex or Petal Base)

to the cake surface, which acts as a temporary glue. This works well on the top surface, but may slip when stencilling the side of a cake.

Prepare the royal icing. It needs to be of a firm peak consistency. Paddle the paste before using it to ensure it is free of any bubbles. Keep the icing covered until ready to use.

Once the stencil is securely in place, apply a layer of royal icing to the stencil using an angled spatula.

Clean and dry the stencil whilst waiting for the icing to dry completely. Then attach the stencil following the above method before stencilling the other side of the cake.

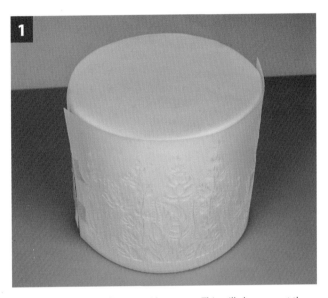

Gently pull the stencil flat to avoid any gaps. This will also prevent the icing from seeping under the stencil.

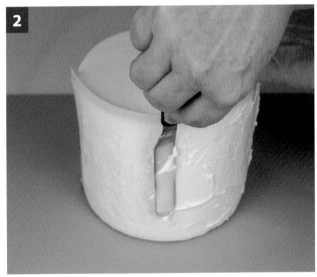

Working from right to left (or left to right if you are left-handed), apply a layer of the icing from the bottom upwards to cover the stencil pattern.

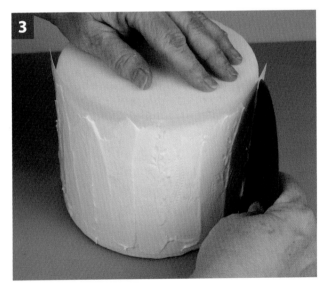

Once the pattern is covered, gently scrape away the excess icing with the palette knife, then use a side scraper for a smooth finish.

Remove one side of the stencil and carefully peel away. If there are any bleeds or peaks in the icing, remove these with a damp paintbrush.

STACKING THE CAKES

Once all the cakes are completely dry and the bottom and middle tiered cakes are dowelled, the cake is ready to be assembled. A firm royal icing is required to act as the 'glue.' When this icing dries, the cake tiers will be very secure.

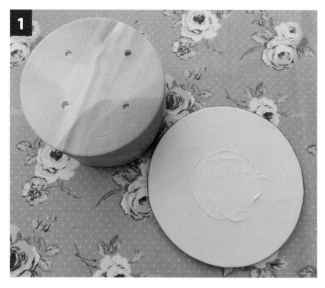

Begin by attaching the bottom tier to the iced board. Apply some royal icing to the centre of the board and then place the cake on top. Use a tape measure or ruler to check that the cake is centred.

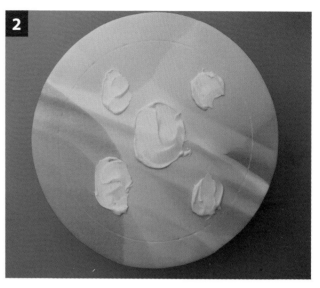

Use an angled palette knife to apply some more royal icing to the centre of the bottom cake. Apply icing over the top of the dowels as well as a little in the centre as shown. Place the middle-tier cake on top, using the score line on the base cake as a guide. Use the ruler to check that the cake is centred, then attach the top tier.

Allow the icing to dry completely before attaching the flowers. Insert flower pics at an angle, and push these into the cake until they are almost level with the cake surface. Trim the stems of the flowers if necessary. Secure the flowers inside the pics with either a little ball of soft sugarpaste or some royal icing.

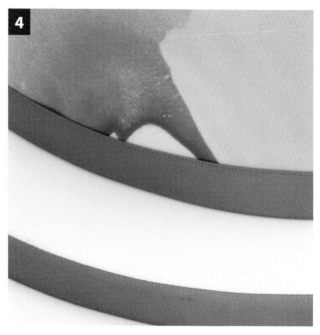

The joins or gaps between the board and the cake as well as between the tiers can either be covered with matching ribbon, or royal icing can be used to pipe a 'snail trail'.

CHAPTER 9

FINISHING TOUCHES

· · · · · · · · · · · · · · · · · · · ·

O nce a cake is covered it usually requires some form of final embellishment. Sometimes all that is required is a ribbon round the base and some candles. Sugar sprinkles, edible shapes and lettering are all readily available to buy in most supermarkets, along with pre-mixed icing for piping. In this final chapter are some suggestions for alternative finishing touches that can be made at home, and how to apply them.

BUTTERCREAM

Different side designs on the cake can be created using either purpose-made side scrapers, known as texture combs, or with a palette knife or spoon. Any type of buttercream can be used to create these effects.

Whichever of the following designs are used, the cake will need to be crumb coated, chilled, and then have a second coat of soft buttercream applied. Smooth over the buttercream with an offset spatula or side scraper to even out the buttercream. It does not have to be perfectly smooth, as it will be textured.

Horizontal grooves.

pressure into the buttercream whilst at the same time rotating the cake. With each rotation, move the spatula slightly higher, until you have reached the top edge of the cake. To decorate the top of the cake, start in the centre and spiral out with the offset spatula whilst rotating the cake on the turntable.

Vertical Grooves

Use the rounded side of a teaspoon to create vertical stripes. Drag the spoon up the height of the prepared cake. The width of the spoon will determine the width of the ridges.

Horizontal Grooves

Place the cake on a turntable. Use the tip of an offset spatula placed at the bottom edge of the cake. Apply

Vertical grooves.

Petal cake.

Texture Comb

Side scrapers are available from cake and craft suppliers. Some have one side smooth and the other has a texture comb. To use the texture comb, prepare the cake as above, but apply the buttercream more generously. Hold the comb so that the bottom is against the cake board. This will ensure the pattern remains in the same place each time the cake is rotated round whilst scraping. After each rotation, add more buttercream if there are any gaps and wipe the comb clean. Continue with several rotations until the pattern is well defined. Use an offset spatula to tidy the top surface.

Piped Side Designs

Petal Cake
Crumb coat the cake and refrigerate for 20 minutes. Cover the top of the cake with a second coat of buttercream and

neaten the edges by using an offset spatula to draw the paste from the edges towards the centre. A swirl pattern could be added to the top using the rounded tip of the spatula, as described above.

Fill a piping bag, fitted with a plain round nozzle. Pipe a row of vertical dots down the side of the cake using a 1.5cm (0.6in) round piping tip (Wilton 1A). Next, spread the buttercream dots with a rounded offset spatula or the rounded edge of a teaspoon, as shown. Pipe another vertical line, and spread the dots again. Continue round until the cake is covered.

Horizontal Ruffle Effect
This is a perfect design for the dress of a dolly cake or a ballerina-inspired cake. For this effect a rose-petal piping tip has been used (Wilton 124 piping tip). Starting from

Using a texture comb.

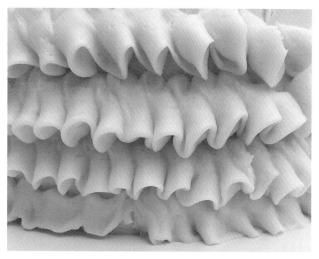

Horizontal ruffle effect.

the bottom of the cake and with the rounded tip at the top, carefully pipe round the base whilst making contact with the side of the cake. Move the bag up and down whilst slowly piping: this will give the ruffle a wavier edge. Piping too quickly will give the ruffle a straighter, flatter appearance. Once the first layer is piped, continue piping another ruffle above and continue piping around and above until the cake is covered.

Vertical Ruffle Effect

For this design, either the same piping tip as above or a slightly smaller rose-petal tip (Wilton 104) can be used. Mark a vertical line on the side of the cake by indenting with a ruler or side scraper to act as a starting point. Start from the bottom, holding the piping bag vertically, with the wider, rounded side of the nozzle against the side of the cake. Work up the side of the cake whilst squeezing the bag gently. Once at the top, push the nozzle into the cake a little to finish off. The more slowly the ruffles are piped, the wavier they will be. Continue piping vertical waves all the way around the cake. Use the angled spatula to neaten the top edge.

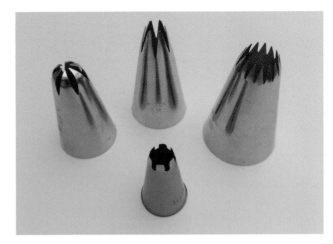

Piping nozzles: from left to right: closed star (2D), open star (1M), open star (6B) and in the foreground, open star (105).

have different numbering codes, making identification a little confusing! For piping buttercream, Wilton piping tips have been used for most of the projects in this book.

The following designs can be used as a border round the top or bottom of the cake. Any of the nozzles shown here can be used, but all will produce a slightly different effect.

Star border

Hold the piping bag at a 90-degree angle and squeeze. Release the pressure and pull away to create stars.

Vertical ruffle effect.

Piping Borders with Buttercream

There is a huge array of different piping nozzles for buttercream available in cake-decorating and craft shops. They are much larger than royal icing tips and are often available in sets. They can be made of metal or plastic. There are several different brands and confusingly they sometimes

Swirl border

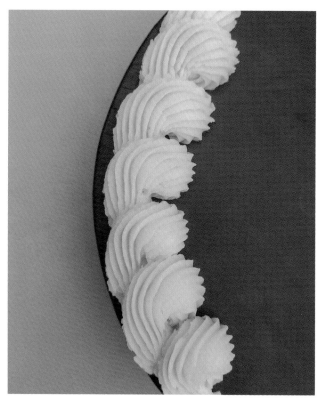

Hold the piping bag at a 45-degree angle. Squeeze with constant pressure whilst moving the piping bag in a circular movement.

Slanted shell border

This piping technique is similar to the shell border, but the piping is slightly slanted towards the centre of the cake.

Shell border

Hold the piping bag at a 45-degree angle, and squeeze. Lift the tip as you pipe the shell, then pull back as you release. The shells can also be piped further apart for an alternative look.

Ruffles swirl border

Hold the piping bag at a 90-degree angle. Gently squeeze and wiggle the bag at the same time, then lift up the piping bag slowly, release the pressure and pull away.

Rosette border

Pipe a rosette by starting on the outside edge and swirling towards the centre of the cake, working from left to right. For the next rosette, pipe in the opposite direction from right to left. Continue piping in alternate circular movements.

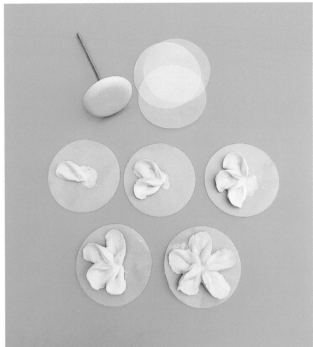

Small wax paper squares and a flower nail are also required.

Piping Buttercream Flowers

Blossom flowers can be piped with buttercream using a 104 petal-tip nozzle. The number of petals can be varied to suit the flower type, but a classic shape and size has five petals.

Place the nozzle into the piping bag before filling with medium consistency buttercream. Attach the parchment square to the top of the flower nail with a little icing. Hold the piping bag with the wide end of the tip towards the centre. Pipe up round and pull down towards the centre whilst turning the flower nail in the opposite direction. Do this action slowly so that each petal is of a consistent size.

These flowers then need to be refrigerated so they can be easily removed from the paper squares before being attached to the cake for decoration. They can also be frozen

Decorate the centres with dragées or sugar sprinkles.

for up to three months. Open freeze first and then decant into a sturdy container to avoid them being damaged in the freezer.

Russian Piping Nozzles

These have become extremely popular in recent years. They produce quite elaborate flowers, and with a little practice are quick to use.

The buttercream required needs to be of a slightly stiffer consistency than usual as this will help the flowers to keep their shape. American buttercream is the easiest to use as it holds its shape and crusts over when set. Use two or three shades of buttercream to create more realistic flowers. Choose a slightly shorter piping bag and do not overfill. Once the nozzle is in place, fill the piping bag, using either one colour or use an angled spatula to coat the inside of the bag and then fill the centre with an alternative colour, as shown in Project 1 in Chapter 3.

Russian piping nozzles come in a variety of designs.

Practise using Russian piping nozzles by piping on to parchment paper first.

Flat-ice cupcakes or crumb coat a larger cake first. Hold the bag at 90 degrees and make contact with the cake surface. Squeeze the bag and at the same time draw the bag up, release the pressure and then lift off. If the icing does not pass through the nozzle, then the icing consistency is too stiff and a little water needs to be added. If the flower flops and does not hold its shape then the icing is too soft and more icing sugar needs to be added to the buttercream. Practise using Russian piping nozzles by piping on to parchment paper first.

MERINGUE KISSES

Small meringues, known as meringue kisses, are a popular piped decoration for cakes. They can be made ahead and stored for weeks in an air-tight jar. The following recipe from 'The Meringue Girls' has been adapted to make a smaller quantity. The mixture uses a 2:1 ratio of sugar and egg whites. 100g (3½oz) of caster sugar and 50g (2oz) egg white will make enough tiny meringues to top a cake. Any spare meringues can be stored for future use.

Preheat the oven to 200°C/180°C fan/gas mark 4. Line a small baking tray with baking parchment and pour in the caster sugar. Heat it in the oven for five to seven minutes.

Whisk the egg whites slowly, allowing small stabilising bubbles to form, then increase the speed until the egg whites form stiff peaks.

Take the sugar out of the oven, and turn the oven down to 120°C/100°C fan/gas 1. With the mixer on full speed, very slowly spoon the hot sugar into the beaten egg whites, making sure the mixture comes back up to stiff peaks after each addition of sugar. Once all the sugar has been added, continue to whisk on full speed until the mixture is smooth, stiff and glossy. If the mixture still feels gritty when rubbed between finger and thumb, keep whisking at full speed until it has dissolved.

Spoon the meringue into a piping bag fitted with an open star nozzle. Hold the bag straight at 90 degrees above the parchment-lined baking tray. Squeeze from 2cm (0.8in) above the tray, and then let go before pulling up to form small peaks.

To create stripes, use an angled palette knife to paint about four or five stripes inside the piping bag with either edible paste colour or some coloured meringue mixture before filling with the meringue mixture.

Bake for about 35–45 minutes or until the kisses come away from the baking parchment easily.

Meringue kisses can be prepared ahead of time and store well.

CHOCOLATE

Decorations can be made using any type of chocolate. The finish will vary depending on whether couverture chocolate is used and whether the chocolate has been correctly tempered. The finish of the chocolate will also vary depending on the type of surface the chocolate is poured on to. If using baking parchment, the chocolate will have a matte finish. If poured on to an acetate sheet the underside will have a glossy finish. Approximately 200g (7oz) of chocolate is enough to make the following decorations for a cake topping. More will be required for covering the sides of a large cake.

Chocolate Shards

These can be used for a decorative topping or a dramatic decoration for the sides of a cake.

You will need:

Chocolate – plain, milk or white
Baking tray, lined with parchment paper or acetate sheet
Angled palette knife

Method:

Melt the chocolate, then pour on to the lined baking tray. Use the palette knife to spread out the chocolate evenly. Leave for five minutes, until the surface is no longer shiny and the chocolate has started to set. Starting from the short edge, carefully roll up the paper. If larger shards are required, do not roll too tightly. Place the roll seam side

Allow to set, before unrolling to reveal the shards.

down on to the baking tray, if using baking parchment. Use either masking tape or a paperclip to secure the acetate roll.

Chocolate Bark
You will need:

Chocolate – plain, milk or white or use a mixture, melted in separate bowls for marbled effect
Baking tray, lined with parchment paper
Angled palette knife
Decoration of choice – freeze-dried berries, dried fruits, nuts, chocolate chips, pretzel pieces, honeycomb, sea-salt flakes or sugar-coated sweets

Method:

Melt the chocolate, then pour on to the lined baking tray. If using two or three different coloured chocolates, pour the dark chocolate on to the tray first and spread over the baking paper, using the angled palette knife. Drizzle over the milk and/or white chocolate. Use a cocktail stick to create a swirled pattern across the chocolate. Break into shards before using. Any unused shards can be stored in a plastic container or bag.

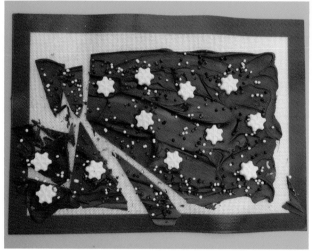

Scatter the decorations evenly over the surface of the chocolate, then leave somewhere cool to set.

Chocolate Twirls
You will need:

Plain tempered chocolate
Baking tray, lined with acetate sheet
Angled palette knife
Small sharp-tipped knife

Carefully unroll the sheet to reveal the chocolate twirls. Pick it up by the edges, to avoid finger marks.

Method:

Melt the chocolate then pour on to the lined baking tray. Use the palette knife to spread out the chocolate evenly. Leave for five minutes, until the surface is no longer shiny and the chocolate has started to set. Starting from the long edge, carefully roll up the acetate loosely and secure with tape or paperclips. Leave to set.

Use a paint-stripping tool to create large chocolate flakes, and a sharp vegetable peeler for small chocolate curls.

Large Chocolate Flakes

You will need:

Melted chocolate – plain, milk or white
Flat baking tray, marble slab or smooth work surface
Angled palette knife
Decorator's paint-stripping knife or large sharp knife

Method:

Spread the melted chocolate on to the clean underside of a baking tray, marble slab or work surface using the angled palette knife. Allow to cool until just at setting point. Hold the stripping tool at a 25-degree angle to the chocolate surface and scrape across to form long flakes. If the chocolate does not curl and breaks, it has cooled too much and needs melting. This can be done by using a hand-held hairdryer or hot gun.

Small Chocolate Curls

You will need:

Thick bar of chocolate at warm room temperature
Sharp, swivel-type potato peeler

This is a very quick way of adding small curls directly to a cake surface. Use the peeler to shave narrow curls from the side of the chocolate bar.

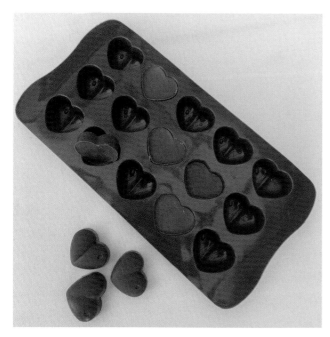

Allow the chocolate to set completely before removing it from the mould.

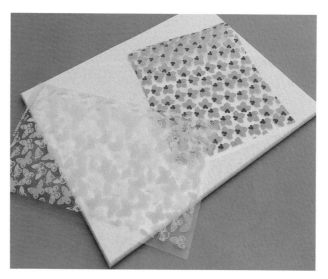

Transfer sheets are available to buy from most cake-decorating and chocolate-making suppliers.

Using Moulds

You will need:

Tempered chocolate, white, plain or dark

Silicone moulds (available from sugarcraft and cake-decorating suppliers)

Method:

Melt the chocolate and either decant into a small piping bag before pouring into the mould, or use a small teaspoon. Setting time can be speeded up by placing the moulds in a fridge or freezer.

Allow to dry flat, before peeling away the acetate.

Chocolate Transfer Sheets

Chocolate transfer sheets are made from acetate with coloured cocoa butter sprayed on to them in a variety of colours and patterns. To use, follow the instructions for making chocolate shards above. Place the transfer sheet on the work surface with the rough side of the transfer sheet facing upwards and shiny side down.

Spread the tempered chocolate over the acetate using an angled palette knife.

Modelling Chocolate and Marzipan

Both these modelling mediums are similar to work with. Both stick to themselves and do not require any glue. Both white chocolate modelling paste and naturally coloured

Chocolate roses made with modelling chocolate are a very attractive decoration for a chocolate celebration cake.

marzipan take colour well by either kneading edible dust or oil-based colour into the paste.

Modelling chocolate and marzipan can be used in silicone moulds and do not require pre-greasing. However, if the moulds are quite detailed, dusting the mould with a little icing sugar or cornflour will help to remove the paste when unmoulding. Alternatively, once the mould is filled, place it in the freezer for five to ten minutes and the shape will be much easier to remove.

Follow the directions in Project 6 in Chapter 4 for making marzipan roses, but substitute the marzipan with modelling chocolate.

Marzipan Teddy Bear Cake Topper

Marzipan for modelling figures is a useful way to use up any marzipan left over from cake decorating. It colours well and can be stored for several months in a cardboard box if not required as a cake topper immediately.

1
Colour some marzipan with either paste or dust-edible colours – chestnut brown and a small amount of black or dark brown. Keep some of the marzipan its natural colour. First damp the hands and have a damp cloth nearby. Take a golf-ball size piece of marzipan and roll it into a ball.

2
Mould the ball into a pear shape, with the widest point at the base. This will be the bear's body. Pinch the top of the 'pear' slightly for the position of the arm sockets.

3
To make the head, roll a smaller ball, then flatten it slightly to make an oval shape as shown.

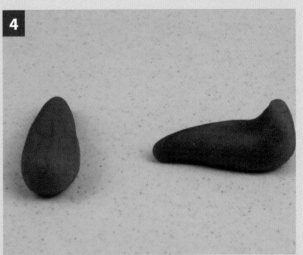

4
To make a leg, roll a marzipan piece into a sausage and taper each end, like a spindle. Make the arms in the same way as the legs, only smaller.

5

For the snout, roll a small ball of natural-coloured marzipan. Flatten and attach to the head. For the eyes and nose, colour some marzipan black, then roll into tiny balls, flatten and attach.

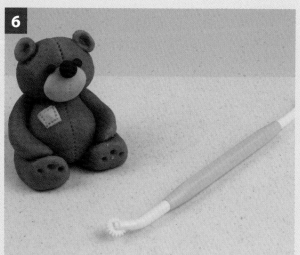

6

Run a stitching tool up the centre of the body, snout and head. Use chestnut paste to make the ears. Use some of the natural paste and the stitching tool to create a little patch.

ROYAL ICING

Royal icing is a classic medium for adding embellishments to a finished sugarpaste-coated cake as well as a royal-iced cake. Numerous designs and effects can be piped by using different piping nozzles. Royal icing nozzles are smaller than nozzles used for piping buttercream. Smaller piping bags made from baking parchment are best to use, as only small quantities of icing will be needed. A smaller bag is also easier to hold when delicate fine detailing is required.

In the photos are some suggested piping tubes made by PME. They are useful for piping simple borders, flowers and lettering. Plain round nozzles are available in sizes 00 up to 4. These are used for piping lines and curves, including lettering.

The most useful sizes for beginners would be nozzles 1, 2 and 3.

Nozzles 42, 43 and 44 are used to pipe shells and ropes.

For piping petals, tubes 56R and 57R are for right-handed people, and 56L and 57L for those who are left-handed.

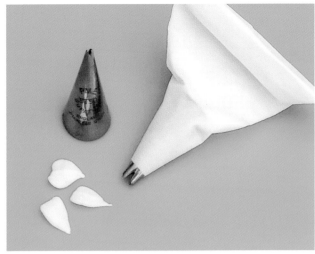

Piping nozzles 50, 51 and 52 are used for piping leaves.

Piped Flowers

For simple five-petal blossoms, follow the instructions for the piped buttercream flowers, but substitute with royal icing, a parchment piping bag, and use either a 56 or 57 piping tube.

Another method for piping flowers is to use a drop-flower piping nozzle. These are available in various patterns and sizes and are a quick way to create small flowers. Firm buttercream could also be used with these nozzles. Line a tray with some baking parchment and secure the corners with a little icing. Insert the nozzle into a piping bag, before filling with firm peak royal icing.

Add tiny sprinkles to the centre whilst the icing is still wet and then leave to dry completely before peeling away from the parchment paper and using.

A Jem 107 drop-flower nozzle has been used here.

Start with your hand twisted slightly anti-clockwise, press the nozzle on to the paper, squeeze the piping bag, turn clockwise, release the pressure and then lift away.

Once dry, the flowers can be stored in a cardboard box indefinitely as long as the environment is dark and dry.

Brush Embroidery

This technique is relatively quick and requires minimal equipment. Originally, the reverse pattern was piped with royal icing on to a Perspex or glass plate, allowed to harden, and then used to emboss the surface of a freshly sugarpasted cake.

'Patchwork cutters' from Marion Frost come in a variety of designs and work particularly well when used for brush embroidery.

Use soft-peak royal icing with a little piping gel added. This will prevent the icing from drying too quickly and allows a longer working time. An alternative medium would

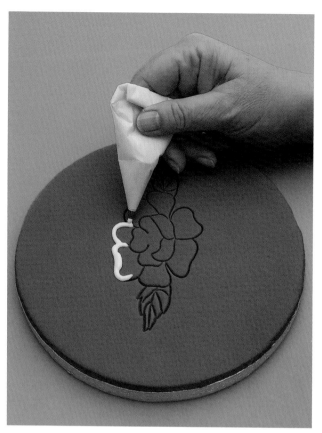

Pipe the outline edge of one petal, then pipe another line on the inside, as shown.

A much quicker and simpler method to emboss a design on to a cake is to use flower and leaf cutters.

Do not press into the sugarpaste too deeply, just enough to create a visible impression.

Continue brushing each side towards the centre.

Brush embroidery flower.

Numbers and large letters can be made by using the run-out technique, as described in Project 15 in Chapter 7. Patterns using alternative royal icing colours can be added whilst the icing is still wet.

Run-outs can also be over-piped once dry to give a more prominent pattern.

Cutters for individual letters and numbers are available from most cake-decorating suppliers, and online. They come in a variety of sizes and font styles. Sugarpaste, marzipan and modelling chocolate can all be used for larger cutters.

This plaque shows a variety of ways to apply lettering to cakes.

be to use sugarpaste that has been mixed with water to create a soft piping paste. Both types of icing benefit from being 'paddled' on to a work board to eliminate any air bubbles and create a smooth icing to pipe with.

Begin by impressing the flower shapes and leaves into the surface of the soft sugarpaste.

Allow the sugarpaste on the cake to dry completely to prevent marking or making any dents into the sugarpaste.

The piping tube size used is dependent on how bold or delicate the finished design is. Piping tubes 1, 2 or 3 can be used. Piping tube 3 has been used here to give a bolder effect. Place the tube into a small piping bag and half fill with icing.

Starting in the centre of the piping, using a small damp paintbrush (size 2 or 3), touch the surface and stroke the icing downwards, towards the centre of the flower.

Dampen and wipe the brush clean as needed, but avoid over-wetting.

Continue to the next flower and repeat.

For the leaves, pipe one side at a time and brush the sides towards the stem.

The central veins of the leaves and flower stems can be overpiped using a no. 1 or 2 piping tube, and the centres of the flowers can be either piped with dots or decorated with sugar pearls.

LETTERING AND NUMBERS

Personalising cakes with lettering is often regarded as an extremely difficult task for an untrained cake decorator, but there are a number of ways to create lettering that do not require direct piping on to a cake.

These run-out letters were over-piped with dots. The heart pattern on the letter E was created by lightly dragging a cocktail stick downwards through the freshly piped icing.

SUGARPASTE/MODELLING PASTE

Sugarpaste is a useful medium for making small cake decorations, which can be easily applied to a cake top. It does not hold its shape very well as it is a soft paste, but when combined with flowerpaste it becomes a firm modelling paste. Different quantities of flowerpaste can be added, depending on how firm the finished modelling paste needs to be. When making ruffles, billows and bows, one third of flowerpaste combined with two thirds of sugarpaste is usually sufficient. The paste will remain stretchy and pliable, but will hold its shape when being applied to the cake.

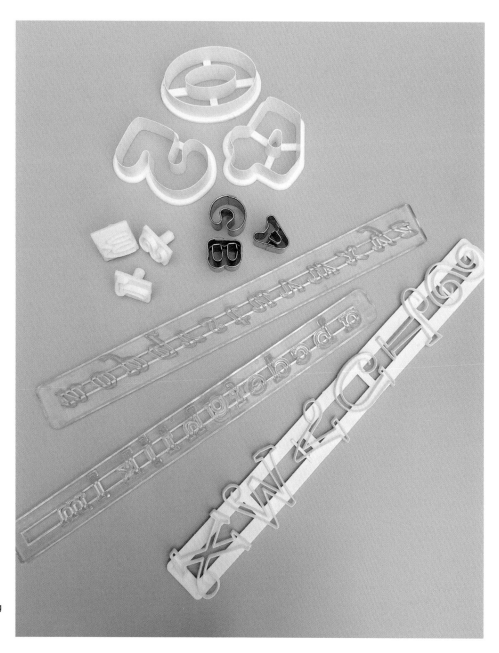

Flowerpaste is needed when using smaller cutters, such as these 'Tappits' from FMM.

Ruffles

To make ruffles for using as a side decoration on a cake, mix the paste as described to make modelling paste and colour with edible paste colour.

Note that approximately 400 ruffles will be required to cover the sides of a 15cm (6in) round cake!

A quicker method for making ruffles round a cake is to cut long strips of modelling paste rather than individual circles. Measure the circumference of the cake and roll out long thin strips of modelling paste with either a pizza wheel or craft knife, or use a wheel cutter. These can then be cut down into shorter strips that are easier to work on, particularly if the cake is large. Place the strip on to a foam pad and frill one long edge, using a large ball tool.

Start at the base and attach the strips, frilled side down, with cooled boiled water or edible glue.

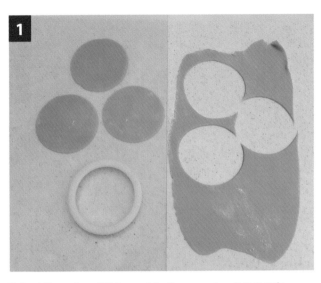

Roll out the paste until it is very thin, then use a 4cm (1.6in) circle to cut out a few circles. Place under a stay-fresh mat, whilst shaping each circle.

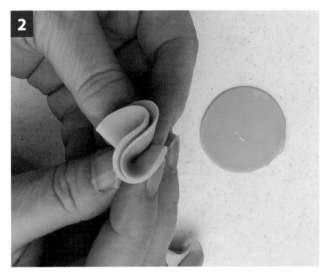

Take the circle, loosely fold it in half, and bend one side forwards and the other side back to create an 'S' shape.

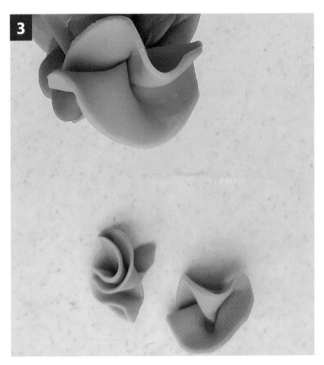

Leave to one side and continue with more circles until you have made enough to go round the base of the cake. Use either royal icing or edible glue to stick the ruffles to the side of the cake.

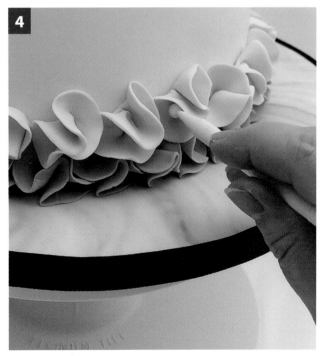

Use a small ball tool placed in the centre of the ruffle to push it on to the cake. Add more ruffles round the base, or even cover the sides of the cake completely.

To create a wave effect, follow the instructions as above for making the ruffles, but use a longer sweeping action with the bone tool to create a smoother, less frilly ruffle. Attach to the cake starting at the top edge and work down the cake. Colouring the paste into three or four different shades will create an ombre effect.

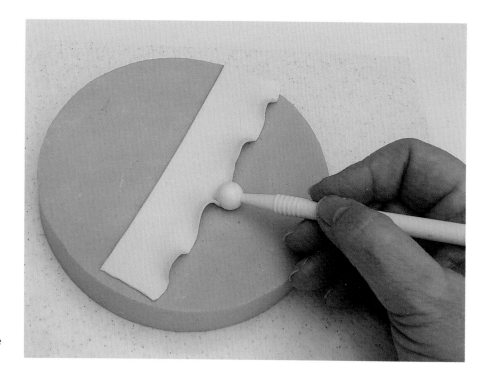

Use a Sugarcraft foam pad, as seen here. The foam is dense, enabling more pressure to be applied to the paste.

For a less ruffled effect, use a larger ball tool and do not apply too much pressure.

Billows

This is another technique using modelling paste that can be used either as a border round the base of a cake or as a complete side covering. You will need a square-shaped cutter, approximately 6cm (2.5in) in width.

Measure the circumference of the cake. For example, a 20cm (8in) cake has a circumference of approximately 62cm (24in), so between ten and eleven squares will be needed for one row of billows. Roll out some modelling paste thinly; use cornflour if the paste is a little sticky.

Use the square cutter, cut out four or five squares, and place under a stay-fresh mat.

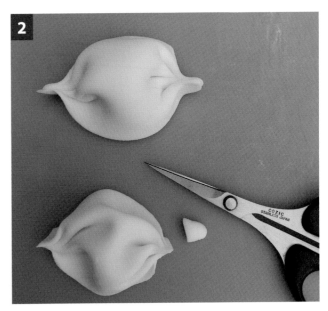

Take one square, moisten the left- and right-hand side of each square and fold both sides concertina style, as shown. Pinch the sides and trim with a sharp knife. Repeat with the remaining squares.

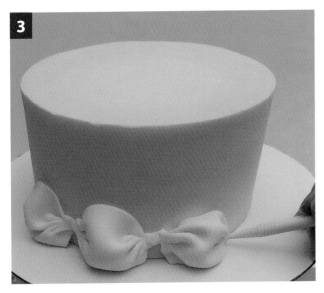

Brush the base of the cake with a little edible glue or water, and attach the billows as shown. Use a small ball tool to push the sides into the cake to secure. Continue making more billows in sets of four and five.

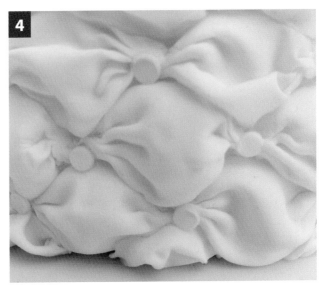

Use sugar buttons or balls between the billows to complete the decoration.

Sugar Bow

A sugar bow on the side or on top of a cake is a popular cake decoration. They can be made in any size.

The bow shown here will suit a smaller cake.

Begin by rolling out some modelling paste quite thinly. Then, using a ruler, measure two rectangles measuring 10 × 5cm (4 × 2in) and cut out. These will become the loops of the bow.

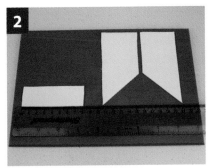

Cut out the middle section of the bow, which measures approximately 3cm (1.2in) wide by 8cm (3in) long. The tails of the bow need to be the same width as the bow loops, 5cm (2in) across. Cut the ends at an angle, as shown. Place all the pieces under a stay-fresh mat.

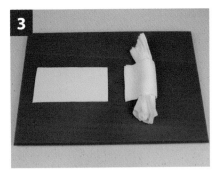

Take one of the bow loop pieces and brush a little edible glue on one of the ends. Twist a square of paper towel into a sausage and lay it across the middle of the paste, as shown. Fold the bow loop round the paper towel.

Hold the joined end, and starting in the middle, fold it backwards and forwards to form pleats, like a paper fan. Brush with a little edible glue to secure the pleats, if necessary.

Repeat to make the second loop. If the bow is to be placed on top of a cake standing up, then place the loops in an upright position at this point.

Trim the ends and brush with a little edible glue before placing the two bow loops together. Allow to dry a little before continuing with the next step.

Take the middle section of paste and form some pleats as shown. Brush some edible glue on the back of the piece and wrap it round the middle of the bow. Trim with a sharp knife and leave to dry.

To make the tails, pleat the ends and attach them to the bow with a little edible glue. If the bow is going to be placed upright on the cake, then add the tails separately. Position the tails on the side of the cake first whilst the paste is still soft, then place the bow on top. If the bow is quite large, secure it with royal icing rather than edible glue.

USING SILICONE MOULDS

Silicone moulds are available from most cake-decorating and craft shops. They are quite expensive to buy, but beware of cheaper moulds that are made from low grade silicone and are therefore not food safe.

Moulds can be used with a variety of ingredients: melted chocolate, sugarpaste, flowerpaste, rolled buttercream, modelling chocolate and marzipan. Some products, such as modelling chocolate and marzipan, are very easy and quick to use as they contain natural oils, making them easy to unmould.

Sugarpaste and modelling paste sometimes require a little dab of cornflour or icing sugar in the mould first. Another technique is to rub a little vegetable fat or petal base into your hands before rolling the paste into a ball and pushing it into the mould. The light covering of fat from your hands is usually enough to help release the shape from the mould.

Silicone moulds are freezer safe, so if using chocolate or a very soft paste, the moulds can be left in the freezer until set and then unmoulded easily. The shapes can also be stored in the freezer, ready to use at a future time. Shapes made from modelling paste or flowerpaste will keep in a cardboard box for months, providing the atmosphere is cool and dry.

Edible Lace

Cake lace has become increasingly popular in recent years, particularly for wedding cakes. Silicone mats in a variety of styles are available to buy from specialist cake decorating and craft stores, as well as online. As with other types of silicone moulds, silicone mats should be purchased from a reputable company to ensure the mats are safe to use with edible products.

The flexible icing is applied in a similar way as a stencil with royal icing, but this icing remains flexible once dry. It can either be used immediately when dry, or be stored in a cake box for weeks, providing the atmosphere is cool and dry. There are recipes available for homemade cake lace, but most use gelatine, making it unsuitable for vegetarians. Ready-made and packet mix flexible icings are easy to use and give a reliable result.

Begin by ensuring the silicone mat is clean and dry. Sift and reconstitute the icing following the packet instructions. Smooth the icing mixture over the mat with either a plastic smoother or a pallet knife. Scrape away the excess and apply another even coat if necessary. Fill in any gaps with the rounded tip of the knife.

For the best results, allow the icing to dry at room temperature for at least six to eight hours. The warmth and humidity of the atmosphere will affect the drying time. Alternatively, place in a cool oven on its lowest setting

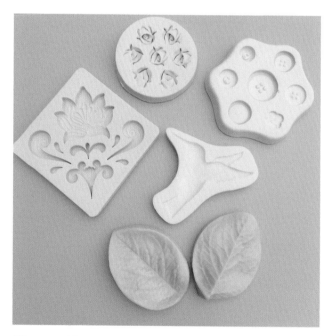

Silicone moulds come in a variety of shapes and sizes.

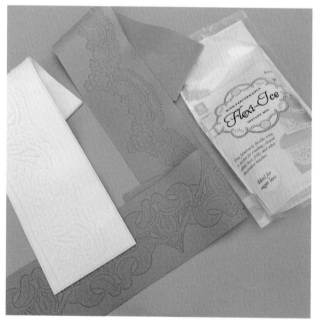

Ready-made and packet-mix flexible icings are easy to use and give a reliable result.

for approximately twenty minutes. Do not over-heat in the oven as the icing will become dry and brittle. If this happens, it can be rescued by covering the icing with a sheet of baking paper, then lay a damp tea towel over the top and leave for ten minutes. When ready, the icing should pull away from the mat easily without sticking. If it is still tacky, then leave it a little longer until it is dry enough to peel away from the mat.

Attach the lace to your cake by brushing the sugarpaste lightly with water or edible glue.

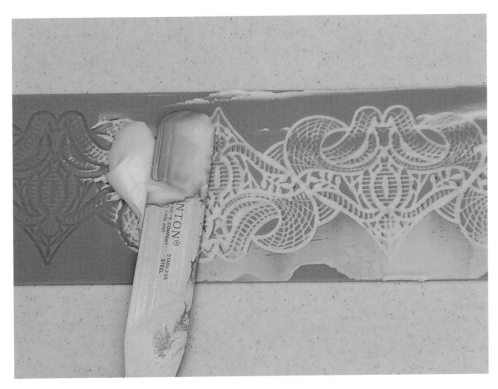

Use a palette knife to smooth the icing over the mat.

Flexible lace can be made ahead of time and stored in a cardboard box. It may become brittle over time, but can be restored by covering with a lightly dampened tea towel.

A wedding cake decorated with white flexible lace. The lace has been embellished with edible sugar pearls.

APPENDICES

· · · · · · · · · · ·

SUPPLIERS

Cake Stuff
Milton Industrial Estate
Lesmahagow
ML11 0JN

www.cake-stuff.com
Baking and cake-decorating equipment including Squires Kitchen products, sugarpaste, marzipan, Callebaut chocolate, cake boards and boxes, stencils and silicone moulds and so on.

The Vanilla Valley
Unit 1, Cardiff Road
Nantgarw
Cardiff
CF15 7SR

www.thevanillavalley.co.uk
Baking and cake-decorating equipment including Squires Kitchen products, sugarpaste, marzipan, Callebaut chocolate cake boards and boxes, stencils and silicone moulds and so on.

Lakeland
Alexandra Buildings
Windermere
LA23 1BQ

www.lakeland.co.uk
Stores throughout the UK and online for baking and cake-decorating equipment.

PME
Knightsbridge PME LTD
Unit 23 Riverwalk Road
Enfield
EN3 7QN

www.pmecake.com/en-gb
Baking tins, baking essentials, stencils and so on.

FMM
Cake Craft Group
Private Road No.8
Colwick Industrial Estate
Nottingham
NG4 2JX

www.fmmsugarcraft.com
Sugarcraft cutters and cake-decorating equipment

Patchwork Cutters
Unit 12, Arrowe Commercial Park
Arrowebrook Road
Upton, Wirral
CH49 1AB

www.patchworkcutters.com
Sugarcraft cutters and embossers.

Buy Wholefoods Online
UNIT B1/B2 Channel View Estate
Laundry Road
Minster
Ramsgate
CT12 4EX

www.buywholefoodsonline.co.uk
Variety of dried fruits and nuts and candied fruits.

IV May Creations
ivmaycreations@gmail.com
www.ivmaycreations.com
www.etsy.com
Artificial flower arrangements for cakes.

Iced Jems
Dudley Road
Stourbridge
DY9 8DU

www.icedjemsshop.com
Cake decorating supplies including piping nozzles, baking cups and cake cases.

FURTHER READING

Sarah's Slice
www.sarahsslice.co.uk/recipes-cakes
Online cake recipes, available to print out.

Jane's Patisserie
www.janespatisserie.com
Three published books and online recipes to print out.

BBC Good Food
www.bbcgoodfood.com
Monthly magazine and online recipes available to print out.

Delicious
www.deliciousmagazine.co.uk
Monthly magazine and online recipes available to print out

Mary Berry
www.maryberry.co.uk
Numerous books for cake recipes, including *Mary Berry's Baking Bible*, *Fast Cakes*, *Mary Berry's Ultimate Cake Book* and *Simple Cakes.*

CONVERSION TABLES

Conversion Table for Oven Temperatures

Celsius (°C)	Fan (°C)	Gas mark	Fahrenheit (°F)
110	90	¼	225
120	100	½	250
140	120	1	275
150	130	2	300
160	140	3	325
180	160	4	350
190	170	5	375
200	180	6	400
220	200	7	425
230	210	8	450
240	220	9	475

Conversion Table Imperial to Metric for Cake Tins

Inches	Centimetres
5in	13cm
6in	15cm
7in	18cm
8in	20cm
9in	23cm
10in	25.5cm
11in	28cm
12in	30.5cm
13in	33cm
14in	35.5cm

Conversion Table for Round and Square Cake Tins

A square tin holds approximately 25 per cent more than a round tin of the same size

Round	Square
15cm (6in)	13cm (5in)
18cm (7in)	15cm (6in)
20cm (8in)	18cm (7in)
23cm (9in)	20cm (8in)
25.5cm (10in)	23cm (9in)
28cm (11in)	25.5 (10in)
30.5cm (12in)	28cm (11in)

Index

First published in 2024 by
The Crowood Press Ltd
Ramsbury, Marlborough
Wiltshire SN8 2HR

enquiries@crowood.com
www.crowood.com

© Claire Fitzsimons 2024

All rights reserved. No part of this publication may be reproduced or transmitted in any form or by any means, electronic or mechanical, including photocopy, recording, or any information storage and retrieval system, without permission in writing from the publishers.

British Library Cataloguing-in-Publication Data
A catalogue record for this book is available from the British Library.

ISBN 978 0 7198 4414 0

The right of Claire Fitzsimons to be identified as author of this work has been asserted by her in accordance with the Copyright, Designs and Patents Act 1988.

Dedication
For my husband, David. Thank you for always supporting me in everything I do.

Acknowledgements
I would like to say thank you to my family, Andrew, Jessica and Callum, who have unwittingly been recipe testers of my various bakes over the years! Thank you to my friends Lin and Angela who have enthusiastically supported me whilst writing this book. Their constant encouragement has certainly boosted my confidence and kept me on track. Special thanks to my friends Liz, who spent hours helping me photograph the step-by-step photographs when I needed two pairs of hands, and Edna for diligently proof reading my endlessly amended texts. Finally, thank you to Clive for producing the most beautiful full-page photographs with such skill and patience. I could not have managed to complete this book without you all.

Image credits
Clive Mumby: front cover, frontispiece, p.8 (left), p.16, p.31, p.35, p.67, p.79, p.95, p.109, p.122.

Typeset by Envisage IT
Cover design by Sergey Tsvetkov
Printed and bound in India by Nutech Print Services